USING HUMOR TO MAXIMIZE LEARNING

The Links between Positive Emotions and Education

Mary Kay Morrison

Rowman & Littlefield Education
Lanham, Maryland • Toronto • Plymouth, UK
2008

Published in the United States of America
by Rowman & Littlefield Education
A Division of Rowman & Littlefield Publishers, Inc.
A wholly owned subsidary of The Rowman & Littlefield Publishing Group,
Inc.
4501 Forbes Boulevard, Suite 200, Lanham, Maryland 20706
www.rowmaneducation.com

Estover Road
Plymouth PL6 7PY
United Kingdom

British Library Cataloguing in Publication Information Available

Library of Congress Cataloging-in-Publication Data

Morrison, Mary Kay, 1946–
    Using humor to maximize learning : the links between positive emotions and
education / Mary Kay Morrison.
        p. cm.
    Includes bibliographical references.
    ISBN-13: 978-1-57886-731-8 (hardcover : alk. paper)
    ISBN-13: 978-1-57886-732-5 (pbk. : alk. paper)
    ISBN-10: 1-57886-731-2 (hardcover : alk. paper)
    ISBN-10: 1-57886-732-0 (pbk. : alk. paper)
    1. Educational psychology. 2. Humor in education. 3. School environment.
I. Title.
LB1051.U725 2008
370.15—dc22   2007042959

∞™ The paper used in this publication meets the minimum requirements of
American National Standard for Information Sciences—Permanence of Paper
for Printed Library Materials, ANSI/NISO Z39.48-1992.
Manufactured in the United States of America.

In loving memory of my father, Bill Wiltz, whose laughter affected the lives of all he touched, especially his sweet cookie: my mother, Ruth Wiltz.

To my loving husband, Don Morrison, who has inspired, encouraged, supported, and loved me. To our children, their spouses, and our precious grandchildren, who enrich our lives with their love: William, Jennifer, Ben, Tyler, Emma, Andy, Julie, Andrew, Mimi, Rachael, Jason, Katie, Peter, Val, Samuel, Christine, Jennifer, and Beth.

CONTENTS

Illustrations   vii

Preface   ix

Acknowledgments   xiii

Chapters

1   Humor—The Tonic for Tired Educators   1

2   Developing Your Humor Being: A Nut Is Born   23

3   Examining Brain Research and Humor: Mouse Droppings   43

4   Hurtful Humor Is No Laughing Matter   71

5   The Humor Workout: Pumping Up with Practice   93

6   Humor Extravaganza: It's a Circus Out There!   117

7   Survival Humor for Stressed Leaders   143

Appendixes

1   Humor Terminology   157

2   Comedian List   163

3   Playful Suggestions   165

4   Sense of Humor Reflections   167

5   Humor Styles Inventory   169

6   Several Categories of Humor   171

7   Humor Belief Inventory   173

8   Humor Terminology List   175

9   Familiar Song List   177

10 Toy List   179

11 Silly Word List   181

12 Bumper Sticker Bombardment   183

13 Take It and Make It—Funny   187

References   189

About the Author   199

ILLUSTRATIONS

Figures

Figure 1-1   Mirthium   8

Figure 1-2   Benefits of humor   10

Figure 1-3   Maslow hierarchy of needs scale   12

Figure 2-1   "No Play"   27

Figure 2-2   Stages of humor development   30

Figure 3-1   Humor enhances learning   44

Figure 3-2   Hook, line, and sinker   50

Figure 3-3   Mouse cages   56

Figure 3-4   Student fears   60

Figure 3-5   School window pain   63

Figure 4-1   Fear factors   74

Figure 4-2   Intent vs. impact   86

Figure 5-1   Nature and nurture elements of humor   97

Figure 5-2   Humor workout cycle   111

Figure 6-1   Three-ring circus   120

Figure 6-2   State changer ideas   136

Figure 7-1   Fun: indicator of a culture of trust   144

Figure 7-2   Framework for learning: humor indicators   145

Tables

Table 1-1   Humergy Characteristics   13

Table 3-1   Cultural Indicators in the Classroom   64

Table 7-2   Worksheet for Analysis of Culture   154

PREFACE

Several years ago I attended the Humor Project's 17th Annual International Conference. Joel Goodman, founder of the project, presented a "Humor in Action: Making a Difference" award to Michael Christensen, the man who founded "Clowns on Rounds." Working in children's hospital wards, these clowns promote healing through humor and laughter. Preceding this presentation was a film clip of these big-hearted clowns interacting with children in an intensive care unit. During the celebration, the comment was made that *where there are children, there should be laughter*. It hit me that I couldn't remember the last time I was in a school and heard much laughter. This was my "aha" moment.

A decade of observations, interviews, and facilitation of workshops coinciding with a passionate interest in brain research have intensified my quest for the connection between humor and learning. This search has allowed me to network with numerous professionals in the medical field. While educators involved in humor research can occasionally be found at the university level, compelling data is emerging in numerous studies from the medical field linking humor, health, and cognitive connections. The opportunity I have had to network and learn from professionals at American Association of Therapeutic Humor conferences, the Humor Conference, and the National Wellness Conference, as well as numerous education conferences, has broadened the scope of this investigation.

People usually choose education as a career because they want to make a difference in the lives of kids. Many find this increasingly difficult. Humor is an overlooked natural resource that can play a crucial role in creating a healthy learning environment, but there is very little written about using humor to meet the escalating challenges that confront educators.

Neuroscience is in the primitive stages of development. The exploding rate of research makes it difficult for even the most committed teacher to stay abreast of this growing knowledge base. Even so, an abundance of research supports the benefits of an enriched learning environment.

Traditionally we do not attend to the brain's biological needs that shape *how* we learn. Learning is nurtured by trusted relationships, strengthened by change, and challenged by the chaos of life. Yet the brains of the children entrusted to us in our schools are required to function in a system that is linear, data-driven, and results-oriented. Thinking is not a valued skill. Standardized tests are given to compare and rank the learning of students. Parents are provided with report cards and letter grades. Except for A students, grades are meant to point out deficits as the way to motivate students to "improve."

This book began during a conversation I had with a colleague about the increasing stress we observed in education. I joked that instead of school improvement, we needed *humor improvement*. As the professional development consultant for leadership in an Illinois regional office of education, I've had immeasurable opportunities to talk with educators. Their frustrations with legislation, bureaucratic paperwork, unfunded mandates, and accountability have created intense anxiety. My initial Humor Improvement Workshops were designed to focus on stress management strategies. In reality, the initial workshops stressed *me*! I lay awake at night wondering if anyone would even attend an all-day session on humor—after all, these administrators and teachers had many more important things to do. How could they find the time to attend with all of the other crucial issues on their plate? If they did come, would they laugh at me, label me "cutesy," and challenge the importance of the topic?

Educators have continued to come to my workshops, and increasingly they request more information about humor. My knowledge has increased along with my confidence. I have learned from their questions, their experiences, and their fears. I have also learned why I was so afraid. Humor is difficult: It is difficult to define and difficult to practice. It is especially difficult to integrate into most school cultures.

The feedback I have received from the workshops has allowed me to reflect on these questions:

☺ How can we use humor to improve the morale in our school?

☺ What are some practical suggestions on how to incorporate humor in the classroom?

☺ Is it safe to use humor with my students only when no one else is around? How can the culture change to support humor?

☺ What is humor, really: nature or nurture?

☺ What is the connection for individuals between humor and learning?

☺ Can purposeful humor impact learning systems? If so, how?

☺ What can be done about negative people who inhibit humor?

Cognitive research continues to clarify my thinking. My focus on humor has broadened from an isolated concept to *mission possible*. We can use humor to create a joyful environment for learning, where humor is not only valued but also an integral component of student learning.

I addressed my own fears by facing the frequent negative reactions to ice-breakers, playful activities, and games. I encountered responses like: "well that may be OK for the elementary grades, but this is certainly not appropriate at our *higher* levels of instruction." Warnings about being too energetic, cutesy, and having too much fun have continued throughout my journey.

My fears have given me insight into all who value humor but are also afraid. The positive responses of educators have ignited my passion for infusing fun into a system that is drowning in the poisons of fear, stress, blame, and punitive measures. I am on a quest to fill the humor void in schools with laughter and fun. This can be accomplished by encouraging further research on the relationship of humor and learning, by being aware of the benefits of humor for all learners (both teachers and students), and by writing a book about what I have learned from a decade of facilitating workshops on humor. We are stuck in a system that ignores what we have gleaned from cognitive science. Our emotions are at the very core of the human experience of learning. The purpose of this book is to explore the links between humor, an optimal learning environment, and the emerging cognitive research on humor development and practice. My purpose is to encourage educators to reach a joy-flow synergy level (see chapter 2) with energy, passion, enthusiasm, and humor as an integral part of their teaching experience. The goal of this book is to ignite the passion of the cultural architects of education to persist in crafting a safe, joyful learning environment filled with *humergy*, the energy of humor.

ACKNOWLEDGMENTS

A huge thank-you to my large, extended Wiltz and Duncan families who have encouraged me. If they all buy a copy it will be a best seller.

A special thanks to my incredible friend Sue Jones Smith, who insisted this book needed to be written, and to Jan Bowman and Kay Poyner Brown who constantly encouraged my creativity. Marcy Mitchell, the administrative assistant at the Regional Office of Education and Dr. Richard Fairgrieves, superintendent of schools for the Boone/Winnebago Regional Office of Education were incredibly supportive. The KIDS (Kishwaukee Intermediate Delivery System) staff were my constant support system during my initial attempts at initiating humor workshops. Evelina Cichy, dean at Kishwaukee College was an incredible mentor and boss and I appreciate my creative colleagues at Kishwaukee College.

Thanks to Dr. Ron Berk for the use of Mirthium and who encouraged my efforts; and to Maylan Dunn, assistant professor of early childhood education at the Northern Illinois University Department of Teaching and Learning. Thanks also to Bob Sylwester, who encouraged my fledgling efforts from the very beginning. I appreciate Bob Nozik, editor for the Association for Applied and Humor Therapy, who reviewed the research, and administrators Gina Swinney, Chris Harris, Mary Ann Kahl, and Jill Gildea, who were willing to read my first drafts and make suggestions. The following folks may not realize how much they influenced my thinking but I am grateful to them: Pat Wolfe, Leslie Yerkes, Kathy Nunley, and Allen Klein. My uncle, Jerry Duncan, contributed to the concept in chapter 1 of the old-time medicine-man show.

My deep appreciation also goes to my first unofficial editor, Jeanne Wyatt, who tirelessly read and reread these passages and gave her patient suggestions. My profound gratitude goes to Bev Letcher for proofreading and for being a wonderfully honest colleague. Thanks to Thomas F. Koerner, editorial director at Rowman & Littlefield Education for his support and to Paul Cacciato at Rowman & Littlefield for his assistance in editing and his patience with a novice writer.

A final note of thanks to all who attended my workshops, endured the games, put up with the jokes, songs, and icebreakers and provided me with the feedback necessary for this book to be written. This includes Principal Pedro Laura and teachers at Dean Elementary School in Woodstock, who were willing to experiment with humor, as well as Principal Becky Girard and the teachers at Maple School in Loves Park. Thanks to Krista Searls, high school English teacher at Durand High School, who shared her research with me and gave me feedback. To all the wonderful folks in the regional offices in Illinois who participated in the power of humor at conferences and workshops—thank you!

Thanks to those who had faith in the power of humor and hired me to be a part of their staff development. Your trust led to this book.

Chapter 1

HUMOR—THE TONIC
FOR TIRED EDUCATORS

"Never take life too seriously, you won't get out alive."

Have you been exhausted, worried, or just plain weary lately? Has the current focus on accountability, data, and unfunded mandates made you irritable? This is your lucky day! Step right up for a sure-fire remedy guaranteed to bring vitality and energy to your teaching. Be prepared to be amazed by the advantages of the humor tonic. But be warned: humor is more than the snake-oil skill of telling jokes. Also be warned that the research contained here focuses on many preliminary findings and could be biased toward the positive benefits of humor. My focus in this book has been to search for the advantages to educators who want to increase humor in their lives. I admit it. I am prejudiced toward the idea that humor is just the tonic needed by educators. So the reviewed studies are presented through my rosy and optimistic lens.

If you want to add a little fun to your teaching, this book is for you! Humor is the real thing. It cures No Child Left Behind blues. It knocks the socks off any bored student. It tickles, splits guts, and generates bellyaches while curing whatever ails you. It might even be funny. Just take a peek at what a healthy dose of humor might do for you! Just a spoonful:

1. Contributes to Mind/Body Balance

> "Worrying is like a rocking chair: it gives you something to do, but it doesn't get you anywhere."

A sense of humor can create a remarkable feeling of control. Learning to use humor as a lens for life challenges can increase your confidence in your own internal ability to adapt. The optimistic energy that comes from humor will enable you to embrace difficulties with resilience. Some people purposefully use laughter to ease pain and promote physical healing. There is some experimental research indicating that laughter and humor might actually cure illness and provide effective therapies for numerous disorders. Some claim that laughter relieves pain, reduces stress, and improves the immune system response (Harvey, 1998). Although these studies are preliminary and no firm conclusions can be made yet, many of the findings are encouraging about the benefits and applications of positive humor.

Got stress? The purposeful use of humor can help you feel more optimistic about your life, knowing that you can choose how to respond to stress. Humor elevates mood and has been known to be a deterrent to depression. Stress reduction is considered one of the most important benefits of humor. A little humor will go a long way in helping educators balance the current focus on accountability, testing, standards, and unfunded mandates.

2. Maximizes Brain Power

> "If you haven't got a sense of humor, you haven't any sense at all."
>
> —Mary McDonald

Humor has the ability to capture the attention of the brain. "Emotion drives attention and attention drives learning" (Sylwester, 1995). Our brain cannot learn if it is not attending. The surprise elements of humor alert the attentional center of the brain and increase the likelihood of memory storage and long term retrieval. Humor has the potential to hook easily bored and inattentive students. It can help the stressed or shy student to relax. As brain food, humor can't be beat.

Word play, puns, stories, jokes, and riddles all involve the creative use of language. Maximizing our capacity to use language through the skillful use of humor will increase the number and speed of the neural connections in the brain. Humor is often used as an indicator for the identification of gifted students.

Just how effective can humor be? The marketing industry gives us an indication. I must confess that I usually watch the Super Bowl just to see the commercials. The money spent for air-time is mind-boggling. Advertisers have less than two minutes to get your attention and put their product into your long-term memory and they spend zillions of dollars to capture the attention of this large viewing audience. Not only do people watch these commercials, but the next day, animated discussion about favorite Super Bowl commercials takes place around office watercoolers. There is a good reason for humor in advertising. An analysis of the retention rate for commercials found that the highest rate of recall was when humor was used (Stewart & Furse, 1986).

3. Enhances Creativity

"Civilization had too many rules for me, so I did my best to rewrite them."

—Bill Cosby

Creativity is the ability of the brain to bring together diverse ideas that will generate the thinking necessary for complex problem solving. Humor and creativity are great companions, each a perfect complement for the other in nourishing thinking. Risk-taking is the nucleus of creativity and of humor; the freedom to express wild ideas activates spirited conversation and sparks the imagination. The creative process flourishes when accompanied by a sense of humor.

Humor increases the potential for divergent thinking and the ability to solve complex problems. By linking previously unconnected areas of the brain, humor forges new associations involving existing concepts. Voila: creativity flourishes.

4. Facilitates Communication

"The person who can bring the spirit of laughter into a room is indeed blessed."

—Bennett Cerf

Using humor to build and maintain relationships is an invaluable skill. Emotional intelligence (EI), the ability to perceive, assess, and influence one's own and other people's emotions is essential for knowing when and how to use humor effectively (Goleman, 1998). The ability to use humor as a part of interpersonal dialogue requires confidence in one's own humor strengths, a fun-loving playful spirit, and the willingness to risk the extraordinary.

Humor generates trust among colleagues and can facilitate a reduction in tension, fear, and anger. Leaders who have the ability to assist others in seeing the "humor" in difficult situations can nurture communication and ease tense situations. Exaggeration, puns, and self-deprecating humor are tools of the trade. Humorists are able to use reframing (example: the ridiculous or exaggeration) as a device to facilitate a shift in context. This shift encourages both individuals and groups to think creatively through shared humor. Laughter can quickly dispel tension and increase the capacity for dialogue.

The use of humor as a tool in communication is rarely taught. It is a skill requiring multifaceted levels of knowledge and ability. Purposeful humor integration provides a distinct advantage in conversation.

5. Supports the Change Process

"Nothing new should be done for the very first time."

There are volumes written about change. Organizational change is a hot topic for school leaders. Whether we encounter everyday small disruptions or a major crisis situation, the way we respond to change varies greatly among individuals and organizations.

Humor can be an indicator of how we are responding to change. It is similar to taking the temperature of an individual or an organization. Our belief systems, our evolved coping skills, our physical being, our temperament, our experiences, our culture, and our gender all combine within our individual neurological system and are all involved in generating our individual response to change. The humor response of any group is a reflection of organizational thinking and can reflect the ability of that culture to adapt.

Our brains crave familiar patterns. We recognize what school bells mean. We understand report cards and grading systems. We are used to a certain structure, procedure, and routine in education. However education has faced increasing pressure from a variety of stakeholders and the demands for accountability have challenged the very core of our system. Change happens frequently, but teachers have an amazing ability to find humor when faced with adversity. Here are some humorous responses from teachers to difficult situations:

- ☺ All teachers must now stay in their rooms until 4:15 p.m. Teachers caught leaving early will be trained in CRAB (criteria referenced abstract bologna).
- ☺ In order to combat obesity, the amount of food in the school lunch will decrease. A price increase of $2 is necessary to implement this change.
- ☺ Research shows that students need more sleep, so homeroom teachers are asked to monitor the amount of sleep their students get. Several teachers have volunteered to sleep during their class period.

Most of us experience unexpected change, suffering, and loss in our lives. When we are able to find the humor in a situation, we can begin to heal and move ahead. Painful experiences, if met with hope and optimism, can produce remarkable growth opportunities. In fact, humor frequently emerges from the downside of our lives. Laughter and tears are closely related, which is why many comedians began their careers by laughing through the tragedy in their lives. This ability for humorous optimism in the face of difficulty is truly a miracle tonic. Change is good—you go first.

6. Creates an Optimal Environment for Teaching and Learning

"You've got to go out on a limb sometimes, because that's where the fruit is."

—Will Rogers

Look for laughter, joy, spirit, and enthusiasm in both the school and in the classroom and you'll find an environment in which learning thrives. Humor contributes to that optimal learning environment. It is brain-compatible both in creating an enriched context for learning and for assisting individuals in the learning process. This is described in depth in chapter three. When you find fun, laughter, and teachers with a sense of humor, learning thrives.

Leadership is correlated with building relationships based on trust. Trust is considered the basis for creating successful learning communities, because it facilitates teamwork and is the foundation for cultivating relationships. A strong bond of trust among members of the school community is essential for school improvement. In *Trust in Schools: A Core Resource for Improvement*, University of Chicago professors Anthony S. Bryk and Barbara Schneider (2002) reiterate the importance of improving the quality of instruction, measuring student performance, and re-shaping education governance. In this groundbreaking study, they cite trusting relationships among teachers, principals, parents, and students as a critical component for success. "We have identified a missing ingredient in the reform recipes: the nature of social practice among adults in school communities and how this is mobilized for sustained school improvement," the authors assert. Their research compares the performance of schools with high levels of trust with those where relationships were not as strong. There was a strong correlation between schools with a high level of trust and top quartile performance on standardized tests.

But what does trust look like? It's simple to observe if you know the indicators. Look for laughter, fun, and joy. When you walk into a building and you can actually feel the joy, you'll recognize the existence of a high level of trust. Humor thrives in an environment of trust and is a major factor that contributes to building trust. When multiple choices are available to an individual within a relationship or within an organization, there are increased opportunities for a sense of humor to thrive. *Fun is an indicator of trust* (Yerkes, 2001).

"Mirthium" is a review of sixty-plus studies conducted over the past forty years, and it gives the reader a clear synopsis of exactly what benefits humor will provide, as well as clarifying some of the existing misperceptions. I am grateful to Ron Berk for his willingness to share his work.

Figure 1-1 is reprinted with permission of Ronald A. Berk (2004) and *Academic Physician and Scientist.* A previous version of "The Prescription Mirthium" appeared at www.ronberk.com/JulAug04_feature.pdf.

DOSES OF HUMOR VITAL FOR EDUCATORS

Noting all the benefits of humor, one would assume that humor studies would be a core component of educator's preservice curriculum. However, the study of humor as a fundamental skill is rarely even mentioned during preservice studies and it's certainly neglected as a topic for continuing professional development.

Even so, it's frequently mentioned as a quality we couldn't do without. For instance, would you want to hire someone without a sense of humor? Of course not. Although humor is mentioned frequently in the literature as exceedingly important and is even considered an essential quality in the hiring process, it's usually neglected as a topic of significant study. As a result of this benign neglect, the exploration of humor in education is a pioneering effort. So, I invite you to take this miracle tonic of humor seriously.

I must caution you: this is not a joke book. While I did a lot of laughing while writing this book, and I obviously think parts of it are pretty funny, the primary intent is not to tell jokes. So, although I hope you will smile and even chuckle as you read, this is not a book with the foremost purpose of making you laugh. This is rather a practical look at a topic that is often ignored in the education world.

The purpose of this book is to affirm, sustain, and encourage educators in the practice of humor not only as a personal tool to optimize a healthy lifestyle, but also to maximize the benefits of humor in education. These benefits include current research-based data on the use of humor to nurture creativity, to increase the capacity for memory retention, to support an optimal learning environment, and to build safe communities that reflect the relational trust necessary for collaborative learning. (See figure 1-2.)

"Oscar makes me take **Mirthium®** *every day before I go to work."*
—**Felix Unger (*The Odd Couple*)**

MIRTHIUM®

(*Generic:* Laughtilyouplotz)

If you have been diagnosed with chronic humor impairment, jocularitis, jesticulosis, or just plain "seriousness," talk to your humor professional about Mirthium®.

Reported benefits are based on randomized, quadruple-blind (even the researcher doesn't have a clue what's happening), placebo, controlled clinical trials worldwide on 7 semi-human HMO CEOs, conducted by several disreputable university researchers. Those results were replicated in studies with 3 blind mice, 5 Chinese hamsters, and a partridge in a pear tree, plus a convenience sample of sheep from New Zealand.

BENEFITS

Based on 60+ studies conducted over the past 40 years, the major benefits are as follows:

Humor

1. Reduces negative emotional consequences of stress, anxiety, and tension
2. Decreases depression, loneliness, and anger
3. Improves mood
4. Increases self-esteem
5. Promotes a sense of empowerment

Laughter

6. Increases pain tolerance and threshold
7. Improves respiration and breathing
8. Improves mental functioning (alertness, creativity, and memory)
9. Exercises facial, abdominal, and thoracic muscles
10. Relaxes muscles/decreases muscle tension

WARNINGS

There are certain claims or common beliefs about the effects of Mirthium® which are false. Research has been conducted on all of the following topics. However, the scarcity of studies, weaknesses in design and execution, or conflicting results render their conclusions as questionable. Seriously, there is insufficient research evidence to support the following claims:

Humor

1. Decreases symptoms of illness and medical problems
2. Enhances interpersonal relationships, intimacy, and marriage satisfaction
3. Increases longevity

Laughter

4. Stimulates the production of endorphins which decrease pain
5. Prevents or alleviates pain
6. Lowers heart rate

Turn over for Side Effects of Mirthium®

Figure 1-1. Reprinted with permission of Ronald A. Berk and Academic Physician and Scientist (September 2006). A previous version of The Prescription Mirthium appeared in Berk, R. A. (2004).

7. Lowers blood pressure
8. Decreases heart disease
9. Decreases stress hormones (serum cortisol, dopac, and epinephrine)
10. Boosts immune system functions to fight viral and bacterial infections and disease
    - ∞ increases immunoglobulin A(IgA), M(IgM), and G(IgG)
    - ∞ increases natural killer cell activity (NKA)
    - ∞ increases number of activated T-lymphocytes (T4 and CD4 cells)
    - ∞ increases T-cell helper/suppressor ratio
    - ∞ increases levels of Complement 3
    - ∞ increases number of B-cells
    - ∞ increases gamma-interferon levels

DOSAGE

Only 1 delayed-release red transdermal patch placed on the tip of your nose with one tablespoon of applesauce every 24 hours. You'll be able to laugh until you're punchy all day and all night.

- ∞ Recommended by the International Association of Polymorphous Prescriptions

- ∞ #1 choice of professors, physicians, administrators, accountants, scientists, engineers, IT specialists, lawyers, IRS auditors, FBI agents, and airport security personnel

- ∞ Immediate results: Start laughing within 3 hours after first dose as the patch dissolves in your nose

CONTRAINDICATIONS

Mirthium® is contraindicated in humans and assorted livestock who have a known hypersensitivity to anything or with nail fungus, a hernia, humongous prostate, cataracts, or irritable howl syndrome. Tell your humor professional about any over-, under-, or around-the-counter medications. Mirthium® interacts with every medication.

SIDE EFFECTS

No severe allergic reactions other than convulsive hysteria and shrieking like a banshee. If laughter continues for more than 48 hours, you should be so lucky. Side effects include: trichinosis, halitosis, gingivitis, hallucinations, drooling, hair loss, athlete's foot, snoring, urge to smoke, malaise (compulsion to eat corn), cavities, gangrene, incontinence, and necrophilia.

QUESTIONS

Ask your humor professional about Mirthium® today. Call 1-555-YO-FUNNY for your free information guide on Mirthium® or visit www.mirthium.com.

BERK PHARMACEUTICALS
(A name you used to be able to trust!)

Figure 1-1. Continued

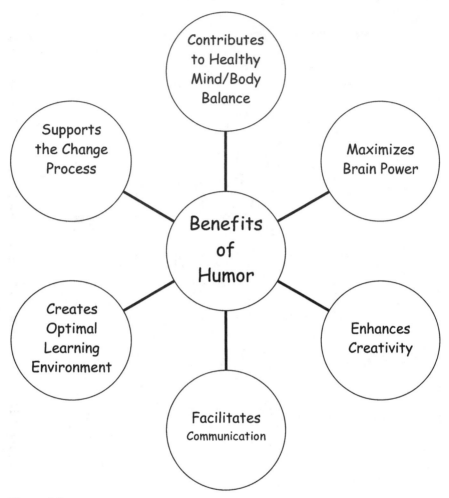

Figure 1-2.

THE ENERGY OF HUMOR/HUMERGY DEFINED

"Analyzing humor is like dissecting a frog. Few people are interested and the frog dies of it."

—E. B. White

At the risk of squashing your interest, clarifying the wriggly aspects of humor is fundamental to the ability to improve our practice. Laughter and humor are related, but not exactly the same (Provine, 2000). Since laughter has such a strong link to humor, a common misperception is that humor is the ability to make people laugh by telling jokes. The ability to tell jokes is a valued skill, but does not begin to explain the complexity of humor.

I'm sure you've heard someone try to describe a funny situation and finally say, "you just had to be there!" Spontaneous group laughter is often impossible to describe. Our ability to laugh with others at the discrepancies of life certainly contributes to our humor experience. Although jokes and funny stories generate laughter, we frequently laugh during normal everyday interactions. When we try to explain to someone else what was so funny, it's difficult to put into words. Phrases that make people laugh are often not very funny when the actual words are examined (Provine, 2000).

Comedy, mirth, stories, wit, and joking are all part of the external experience of laughing with other people. However, humor experienced with others is different than our own unique sense of humor. It is essential to distinguish between the two.

The dictionary definition for humor is as follows: "humor is the quality that makes something amusing or laughable."

The word humor by itself, without any sense as in "sense of humor," is defined in the dictionary as the quality that makes something amusing or laughable. Humor by itself then, is that which would be considered to be funny. When you bring a sense to humor a metamorphosis occurs.

A sense of humor is the capacity of a human being to respond to life challenges with optimistic enjoyment (Morrison, 2005).

Just because laughter is a universal human trait does not guarantee that there exists a universal understanding of humor. Cognitive, emotional, behavioral, psychophysiological, and social components are all factors of humor (Martin, 2001). The multifaceted nature of humor can pose numerous challenges for valid research. At the risk of oversimplifying the complexity of humor, the above-mentioned definitions will be used in this book. Additional definitions are found in appendix 1: Humor Terminology.

Our individual sense of humor is inseparable from our whole being. It is intrinsically woven into our emotional and social psyche and reflects our ethics and belief systems. The ability to adapt to change with enjoyment or at least a positive acceptance defines the essence of having a sense of humor.

JOY-FLOW EXPERIENCES

"Age doesn't always bring wisdom, sometimes age comes alone."

Enthusiasm, energy, joy, and hope merge to create the peak experiences most of us identify with a sense of humor. The relatively new field of positive psychology strives to understand and promote the human potential that enables individuals and communities to thrive. Humor is one of the complex cognitive strengths that connect our basic temperament and our lifetime experiences. The energy of humor, or "humergy," is an indicator of reaching the "self-actualization" level on Maslow's Hierarchy of Needs Scale (Maslow, 1968) as shown in figure 1-3.

Maslow generalized that self-actualizing people tend to respond to life challenges with a spontaneous and creative personality. He defined profound moments of joyful understanding as peak experiences with

Figure 1-3.

heightened sensory experiences integrating hope, optimism, and peace. It's difficult to find specific terminology that expresses Maslow's peak experience. The vitality of humor energy that emerges from a hopeful, joyful spirit of humor needs defining. I call this peak experience of a vigorous, optimistic energy *humergy*.

Humergy is the energy that emerges from the joy and optimism of our inner spirit, reflects our unique personality, and nourishes a healthy mind/body balance. It's possible to clarify the characteristics that inhibit humergy and those that promote its development, as shown in table 1-1. Stress, fear, and pessimism hinder the ability of an individual to enjoy the fullness of a humergy lifestyle. Healthy relationships, optimism, and an environment of trust nurture the growth of humergy.

This energy is being explored in the newly defined field of positive psychology, which addresses the study of positive emotions. Richard Davidson's research on "approach-related positive emotion" characterizes certain individuals as having enthusiasm, alertness, energy, and persistence in goal orientation (Davidson, 2000). The purpose of positive psychology is to understand and promote the human strengths that enable individuals and communities to thrive.

The Positive Emotions and Psychophysiology (PEP) Lab at the University of Michigan is conducting one of the most fascinating projects in studying positive emotions. The research is based on the belief that positive emotions extend the capacity for attention, cognition, and action. The goal of the PEP Lab is to focus on how positive emotions enable human beings to "flourish." When positive emotions are absent, people lose their freedom of choice, they stagnate, and are predictable. When there is ample supply of positive emotionality, people are creative, resilient, and unpredictable (Fredrickson 2003).

Table 1-1. Humergy Characteristics: Developmental Humergy Characteristics of Individuals

Humor Inhibitors	Humor Developers
Stressful relationships	Healthy relationships
Low self-confidence	Self-confidence
Authoritarian environment	Trust: risk-taking environment
Anxiety, fear of fun and play	Joyfulness, playfulness
Helplessness	Hopefulness
Pessimism	Optimism

🔲 Jest for Fun 🔲

Pioneering efforts are being made by counselors and psychologists to incorporate humor into therapy treatments for patients. The use of humor in the medical field was highlighted in the movie *Patch Adams*, the story of Hunter Adams, who promoted the use of humor as a medical practice. His goal was to fulfill his patients' fantasies, ease their fears, and increase their endorphin levels. Several organizations promote humor research.

> The International Society for Humor Studies (ISHS) is a scholarly and professional organization dedicated to the advancement of humor research. Many of the Society's members are university and college professors in the Arts and Humanities, Biological and Social Sciences, and Education. The Society also includes professionals in the fields of counseling, management, nursing, journalism, and theater. All of our members are interested in humor's many facets, including its role in business, entertainment, and health care as well as how humor varies according to culture, age, gender, purpose, and context. (www.hnu.edu/ishs)

A notable organization that promotes humor is the Association of Applied and Therapeutic Humor (AATH). This organization is open to all who are interested in promoting the positive benefits of humor. AATH defines humor as "any intervention that promotes health and wellness by stimulating a playful discovery, expression or appreciation of the absurdity or incongruity of life's situations. This intervention may enhance health or be used as a complementary treatment of illness to facilitate healing or coping, whether physical, emotional, cognitive, social, or spiritual" (www.aath.org/).

Another organization that focuses on humor was founded by Joel Goodman. "The HUMOR Project, Inc. is the first organization in the world to focus full-time on the positive power of humor. The Humor Project mission is to make a difference by being a unique, pioneering, and cutting-edge organization that touches the lives of individuals, organizations, and nations. They seek to help people get more smileage out of their lives and jobs by applying the practical, positive power of humor and creativity" (www.humorproject.com/about/).

"A humorist facilitates the capacity of others to adapt to everyday or to global change, with laughter and feelings of hope and optimism."

—Mary Kay Morrison

A HISTORY OF FUNNY

"The kind of humor I like is the thing that makes me laugh for five seconds and think for ten minutes."

—William Davis

In addition to Maslow, an odd assortment of characters from history provide insights into our current understanding of humor. It is claimed that humor was invented in the 1400s by Duke Knock of the Knock who was trying to ascertain why doth ye chicken traverse ye thoroughfare. Others assert that humor was invented by Al Gore to alleviate boredom with politics. Actually, the word humor is derived from the Latin word umor which means fluid or moist. The role of early medicine was to keep the humors in balance.

Hippocrates clarified the Greek idea of four humors, which were related to temperament and disposition. In the 1600s it was determined by physicians that four liquids called humors determined a healthy balance of mind and body. These were blood, black bile, yellow bile, and phlegm. An imbalance of humors signaled abnormal behavior or mental illness.

During the Renaissance period, "humorous" actually referred to anyone who was considered demented. In fact, it was not until the 1700s that humor was considered normal behavior. Puritans actually forbade the use of most comedy, play, and fun. Some think that this negativity towards humor persists in several forms today.

Shakespeare contributed to an understanding of the terminology *comedy* and *tragedy* through his literary works. Comedy was not really "humorous," but depicted ordinary characters who would triumph, while tragedy involved great characters who made mistakes or suffered painful experiences often resulting in death. Shakespeare interspersed comedy and tragedy with an emotional impact that has survived over the years and still remains as an important work in most school curricula.

Charlie Chaplin, known as the tramp philosopher, began his film career with the release of a silent picture, *The Tramp* (1915). He energized audiences with his tragicomedy portrayal of a little guy against the world. He focused his work on the premise that people can and should laugh at life's tragedies.

Mark Twain, born Samuel Clemens in 1835, is known as one of the greatest American humorists. Twain wrote *The Adventures of Tom Sawyer* and *The Adventures of Huckleberry Finn*, both examples of finding humor in everyday life. His literature has long been a familiar staple on the reading lists for elementary students.

> "Suppose you were an idiot and a member of Congress. But I repeat myself."
>
> —Mark Twain

Will Rogers, born in 1879, had top billing with a vaudeville act in the renowned Ziegfield Follies. As a syndicated column writer, he intertwined humor, current events, and human idiosyncrasies, and his ability to poke fun at politicians endeared him to the American public. His career included work in the movies and he became a well-known figure. His quotes are still applicable today.

> "There's no trick to being a humorist when you have the whole government working for you."
>
> "Be thankful we're not getting all the government we're paying for."
>
> "Everything is changing. People are taking their comedians seriously and the politicians as a joke."
>
> "I don't make jokes; I just watch the government and report the facts."

Abraham Lincoln was known for his animated storytelling. His clever wit was often used to disparage political opponents. His most engaging quality was the ability to laugh at his own physical imperfections, a trait that endeared him to the American public.

"If I were two faced, would I be wearing this one?"

"Common looking people are the best in the world; that is the reason the Lord made so many of them."

Norman Cousins is the person credited with the initial research on the relationship between laughter and wellness. He wrote about his experiences in his best-selling book, *Anatomy of an Illness as Perceived by the Patient: Reflections on Healing and Regeneration*, published in 1979. His personal story of a life-threatening illness and his belief that laughing would help him to heal has become legendary. He checked himself out of a hospital and into a motel to watch funny movies as part of his therapeutic process. He recovered fully and decided that humor was a major part of his healing process.

Lucille Ball captured the hearts of the world with her portrayal of an everyday housewife who turned ordinary events into an extremely funny sitcom. She had an enormous impact on the transition of the media from movies to television and was one of the first women to become a nationally known television star.

"The secret of staying young is to live honestly, eat slowly, and lie about your age."

"You see much more of your children once they leave home."

Bob Hope performed in radio, movies, and television and became famous for his one-liners. He is cited by the Guinness Book of Records as the most honored entertainer in the world. He performed for the American military troops stationed overseas and won the hearts of the soldiers during those performances with his ability to help them laugh at their own difficult situation.

"If you haven't any charity in your heart, you have the worst kind of heart trouble."

"A bank is a place that will lend you money if you can prove that you don't need it."

"I love to go to Washington, if only to be near my money."

Bill Cosby has touched people's lives by providing humorous insights into everyday situations of parenting and family life with his television sitcom. As an author and speaker, he continues to share his wit and insights. Recently he has used his comic visibility to espouse his opinions about controversial racial issues. These are not laughing matters to Cosby, who strongly advocates views that are not typically verbalized. He uses humor to communicate the following:

> "A word to the wise ain't necessary—it's the stupid ones who need the advice."

> "Always end the name of your child with a vowel, so when you yell the name will carry."

> "Let us now set forth one of the fundamental truths about marriage: the wife is in charge."

Erma Bombeck was a journalist who wrote a weekly humor column focusing on life as a parent. Her books became best sellers and often focused on helping parents laugh at the challenges of having children. When she became a cancer survivor, she helped many learn to laugh through this illness. Her courage and ability to laugh during her cancer battles continue to inspire those suffering from terminal illness.

> "Humor is a spontaneous, wonderful bit of an outburst that just comes. It's unbridled, it's unplanned, and it's full of surprises."

> "If you can't make it better, you can laugh at it."

Johnny Carson, David Letterman, and Jay Leno have helped many Americans end their day with laughter. Late night television is a way of life for many Americans. Often the humor revolves around current political situations. The format allows us to laugh at the unusual things national figures say and do. Letterman's top ten list has become a part of American culture and is included in this book as a strategy to teach various aspects of humor.

The list of comedians who have influenced my understanding of humor is immeasurable. An expanded list of comedians is in appendix 2: Comedian List and can be used for several of the activities described in this book. The reader will have their own favorite comedian, but these individuals have most influenced my comic insights.

> "A humorist is a person who feels bad but who feels good about it."
>
> —Don Herold

 ## Jest for Fun

Pick a humorist who makes you laugh. Search the web for their bibliography and famous quotes. Post your findings on the staff bulletin board. (See appendix 2: Comedian List.)

THE TONIC OF HUMOR IS CONTAGIOUS—CATCH IT!

The tonic of humor is available free of charge and the side effects are laughter and fun. The joy-flow experience of humergy is observed when enthusiasm, excitement, and energy are bubbling from individuals who are passionate about their work. This synergy is experienced in an environment that is humming with the spirit of joyful learning. Humergy is reflected in the excitement of students and teachers as they exude a zest for life and a quest for knowledge.

SUMMARY

There are numerous benefits derived from humor. Humor is an oft-overlooked skill that has many benefits, including providing stress relief, maximizing brain capacity for learning, increasing creativity, improving communication skills, and creating an environment of trust. Humor is inseparable from our whole being. It is intrinsically woven into our emotional and social psyche reflecting our ethics and belief systems.

The numerous definitions of humor include what makes you laugh or is amusing. However, a sense of humor is the capacity of a human being to respond to life challenges with optimistic amusement. There is a synergy evident in people who have such an optimistic sense of humor. *Humergy* is the energy that radiates the joyful optimism of our inner spirit, reflects our unique personality, and nourishes a healthy mind/body balance (Morrison 2005).

When there is a fusion of enthusiasm, energy, joy, and hope, a peak experience emerges that most of us identify as a sense of humor. The relatively new field of positive psychology strives to understand and promote the human potential that enables individuals and communities to thrive. Humor is one of the complex cognitive strengths that emerge connecting our basic temperament and our lifetime experiences.

Many people and organizations have contributed to the field of humor. Humorists purposefully and deliberately use humor to focus on truth. Effective leaders understand that the energy of humor is a sign of a healthy organization built on trust.

Powerful Practice—Strategies for School Leaders

- ☺ Staff meeting activity. Post humor definitions from a variety of sources on the walls. Participants choose the definition that most closely aligns with their belief, then physically go and stand by their choice. The gathered group will discuss why they chose that quote. They can report their discussion highlights to the rest of the staff. This is a good activity for an initial discussion on differing humor beliefs. (See appendix 1 for definitions.)
- ☺ Expand the humor selection in your staff library. Encourage discussion and sharing of joyful practice. Be sure to include resources for both students and staff.
- ☺ Encourage flexibility in workplace norms. When you provide the freedom for individuals to accomplish their work within their own time frame, you are letting them know you trust them as professionals. The rigid imposition of rules (such as you must stay in the building until 4:00 p.m.) decreases the ability for fun and laughter and increases the likelihood of low morale. Allow access to the building over the weekend and other times so work can be accomplished within the educators' time frame.
- ☺ Provide the opportunity for staff to discuss this book, as outlined in the first section of the study group format. Invite participation and encourage attendance with prizes, food, and fun.

☺ Invite staff members to share the funniest thing that has happened to them as a teacher. Compile these into a memo that is sent to the other schools in the district, inviting them to compile their own stories. Publish a district book of student/teacher funnies, keeping names anonymous.

Study Group Focus

Divide faculty into five teams to research the benefits of humor.

1. Have the first staff meeting of the month devoted to one of the benefits of humor. Each group integrates the benefits of humor at staff meetings and incorporates humor all month.
2. Publish each of the benefits of humor in the school newsletter. Highlight examples of individuals exemplifying these benefits with connections to the benefits for learning.
3. Contact the media to show how the school is using the benefits of humor to create an optimal environment for student learning.

Study and research the concept that fun is an indication of trust.

1. Conduct a survey with students and staff to find out the beliefs about humor in your workplace. Compile survey results and discuss.
2. Identify and celebrate the areas of humor strength that currently exist both on an individual and a collegial basis. List the ways your staff and students currently have fun. Build on your strengths.
3. Brainstorm ways to increase the fun/trust opportunities that will optimize student learning. Develop an action plan.

Café Conversations

☺ Discuss your favorite historical contribution to the field of humor. How could this information contribute to the improvement of student learning?
☺ Review Maslow's hierarchy of needs scale (figure 1-2). Is it possible to continuously sustain the peak experience stage?

☺ How does the field of positive psychology correspond to the field of education?

"Eat a live toad in the morning and nothing worse will happen to either of you for the rest of the day."

Chapter 2

DEVELOPING YOUR HUMOR BEING

A Nut Is Born

"Today's mighty oak is just yesterday's nut that held its ground."

In a nutshell, humor is a fundamental and integral core of our cognitive emotional growth. The fertile ground of trust and the elements of nurturing relationships are required for humor to take root. How can parents and teachers nourish the little nuts that are searching for the ground in which their humor can flourish?

Each nut has the capacity for humor development and studies of early humor development reveal universal patterns of growth. Each child is born with a unique disposition. Although essential questions revolve around the relationship between the environment and the humor developmental process, there are significant factors that support optimal humor maturation.

While it is understood that children are born with an inherent predisposition for temperament, the environment significantly impacts our nuttiness. Let's look at both the nature and nurture of humor maturation.

NATURE OF THE NUT

Are we born with our sense of humor? A glimpse into the research on temperament provides convincing evidence that some of our humor characteristics emerge from our biologically based temperament. Our innate individual differences usually remain somewhat stable through-out our life and impact the way we respond to our environment.

If you are the parent of more than one child, you will have noticed in-dividual differences between siblings from birth. There are nine tem-perament characteristics detailed in *The Temperament Perspective* (Kristal, 2005). Each infant has a different degree of each of the identi-fied characteristics. A few of these are worth noting because they can impact our humor style and humor growth.

Intensity is the reactive energy of a response, whether happy, sad, or angry; that is, how expressive a child is. The emotional response varies greatly among young children. For instance, some children will smile a little at peek-a-boo games while others laugh loudly.

Adaptability describes how easily a child adjusts to changes and tran-sitions. A sense of humor is closely related to our flexibility for change. The ability to laugh in new situations is apparent even with very young children. Some are at ease right away while others may hide behind a parent when in a new situation.

Mood is the basic quality of disposition. It may be more positive (a happy or cheerful child) or more negative (a cranky or serious child). Some researchers think that mood is a parallel characteristic or that it overlays our basic temperament.

Approach/withdrawal is the child's initial response to novelty: new places, people, situations, or things (Kristal, 2005). It takes a certain de-gree of risk-taking to experiment with humor. Class clowns for instance are pretty comfortable with new places and situations. They approach situations with enthusiasm, zest, and unbridled risk-taking.

Our moment to moment experiences contribute to our current feel-ings and are based on the presence or absence of certain chemicals in the brain. As feelings fluctuate, our emotions are somewhat restricted to the range and scope of our innate temperamental structure.

What influences our individual humor style? While our temperament forms the basis for the energy of our humor style, we can increase our hu-

mor capacity with intentional efforts. Understanding our own temperament contributes to our ability to maximize the development of our own
unique humor style and humor strength. Details on humor strength and
style are included in chapter 5 of this book. However, I encourage you to
think about how your basic temperament has shaped your "nuttiness."

 **Jest for Fun**

Observe your colleagues and try to identify their temperament. What type
of humor is exhibited by those who are bold risk takers versus those who
may tend to be more reserved?

NURTURING THE NUT

Experiential play is a critical component for learning. Play encourages
the discovery skills that generate neural connections while promoting
creativity, critical thinking, risk taking, and social bonding. Free play in
the classroom is child directed rather then adult directed. Choice, risk
taking, and exploration are the foundation for humor development and
are a basis for learning through play.

The experience of play is critical for a child's initial understanding of
the world and a necessary foundation for reading skills. As Ricki Linksman of the National Diagnostics Reading Institute suggests, the pre-
school years are the time for children to develop all learning modalities
through a variety of experiences including visual, auditory, tactile, and
kinesthetic modalities. Providing play centers with choices for young
children will enable them to engage in activities that will develop the
prereading skills needed for every child to become a successful reader
(Linksman, 2007).

There is a dedicated "play" circuitry in the brain equivalent to the cir-
cuits of fear and love (Panksepp, 2003). In studies of juvenile rats, it was
found that play strengthens the social connections between the young
rodents by producing signals, which Panksepp believes are similar to human laughter. Playing contributes to how young mammals build a memory base in the brain. In mammals, vocalization sounds emerge from
tickling and roughhousing activity. In humans this vocalization is called

laughter. Laughter is a human response to a social connection (Provine, 2000). Our emotional systems are designed to share feelings expressed verbally or through facial expressions and body language. Play strengthens these social connections.

Physical strength, mental agility, and social skills improve with play. Children laugh often during early childhood. There are references to the number of times that adults laugh as opposed to the frequency of childhood laughter, but claims that children laugh more frequently then adults have not been substantiated (Martin, 2007).

Two studies show supporting evidence for the link between human play and learning. In a fascinating look at the role of play and its effects on primate learning, Lee Alan Dugatkin (2002) suggests that research is pointing to play in childhood as a means of learning to handle unexpected events in adulthood. It is possible to better prepare an individual for everything from disappointment to physical error, from submission to dominance, from reading social cues to knowing social limits. In humans, measures of rough and tumble play in childhood correlate with scores on social problem-solving tests. In addition, "the neural circuitry of play suggests a potential link between play and learning." Although this theory has been explored and supported many times before, it has been through the study of the frontal lobe.

Now, there may be indications that play increases the versatility of choices, either in decisions, emotional reaction, or physical movement. It may mean creating a repertoire of sensorimotor experiences that can be used as measuring sticks for effective response choice in the future.

By *renaming play as exploratory time*, Steven Wolk (2001) emphasizes the importance of self-discovery, and of having the student in control of his or her own learning. Wolk asserts that during exploratory time children build the cognitive skills needed to accelerate learning.

🔲 Jest for Fun 🔲

Colleagues can list on an index card their favorite way to play. A name or a code is written at the bottom of the card. Shuffle the cards and each person draws one. Cards can be read out loud with guessing as to who wrote the card. Or folks can find a partner and have time to share twice; once as the player and the second time as the play teacher. Actual play is encouraged. (See figure 2-1.)

Figure 2-1. We might as well put this on the entrance to our schools!

"I want to live forever. So far, so good."

PLAY AND PREJUDICE

The belief that play has no place in the serious business of education has been woven into the fabric of our system. The very word "play" is repulsive to some people in education, who think of it as the antithesis of learning. We compel young children to "do worksheets" rather than allow cognitive growth through the natural exploration that play provides. Ask a young child their favorite subject and "recess" becomes the increasingly frequent answer as children progress through school. Learning is perceived as "work." Recess is often the only time that children have free choice. Play is a critical component for humor development, yet the opportunities for play in our educational systems are near extinction for both children and adults.

Play is often considered to be suitable only for very young children. When using the word "play," I have actually had it trigger an intense negative reaction. There are those who express a disdain for the use of any

activities perceived as "okay" for elementary and early childhood educators, but certainly not appropriate in the "higher" cognitive processes
necessary after fifth or sixth grade. "Conventional" wisdom dictates a
general belief that students need to buckle down, work harder, play less,
and quit clowning around as they grow. As children advance through
school, auditory methodology increases, so that by high school many
classes are in a lecture format with few games and activities. Therefore
high school and middle school teachers have immense obstacles to overcome in providing opportunities for play. These obstacles need to be addressed by increasing the awareness that humor facilitates learning, play
encourages memory retention, and laughter relieves the stress that in-
hibits cognitive processing. Research on these factors will be explored in
depth in chapter 3.

Previous education practice was often founded on the belief that
learning is exhibited by sitting quietly, listening, note taking, and rig-
orous testing. However, many teachers are adapting their curriculums
to reflect current cognitive research on learning. It is a true measure
of commitment for an educator to leave the safe structures of the
past, confront any fear they may have, and be willing to adapt their
practice as cognitive research changes our thinking about teaching
and learning.

SO PLAY AROUND!

The motivation to play and laugh is innate to the human species
(McGhee, 2002a). Young children play and laugh even without efforts to
nurture these behaviors. Widespread differences in the development of
humor skills can be seen as children grow older. Increased opportunities
for humor development will foster key intellectual, social, and emotional
life skills.

Integrating play into classroom practice is a purposeful, challenging,
and splendid responsibility. It also brings great satisfaction. Don't be
afraid of being silly or looking ridiculous. Have courage. Live on the
wild side with the purposeful inclusion of humor and fun in your personal and professional life.

Actually there are numerous companies who have been experimenting with the concept of play as a means to empowering employees and tapping into their creativity. Think tanks, meditation rooms, team building activities, and actual opportunities to use toys have found their way into boardrooms and businesses. Companies have found increased productivity with increased opportunities for fun (Yerkes, 2001). See appendix 3: Playful Suggestions.

 Jest for Fun

Have a toy bag that you bring with you everywhere. Find ways to grow your own "child within" by using these toys frequently. Share toys in your classroom with the students. Have a discussion about playfulness. Use a toy as a story starter. (See appendix 10: Toy List.)

As a child develops, the chemical composition of the brain combines with positive environmental factors to cultivate a sense of trust. A feeling of control over one's environment (with choice) gives hope to individuals in their inherent determination to reach developmental goals. Trust and hope provide a basic foundation for developing a sense of humor and there is a pattern of humor development that can be recognized, nurtured, and cultivated. The idea of humor developmental stages has been developed by researchers D. H. Fuhr, Paul McGhee, E. A. Schwartz, and Avner Ziv. As with any maturational sequence, characteristics of these stages are flexible and there will be variances as to when the growth of the emerging nut occurs. (See figure 2-2.)

GROWING UP FUNNY:
AGES AND STAGES OF HUMOR DEVELOPMENT

These stages of emotional progression are observed most often through play and are the essential foundation for the development of a sense of humor. Hope, trust, positive emotionality, and optimism are integral to the maturation process. I have identified each of these stages by a prevalent game or activity of the stage.

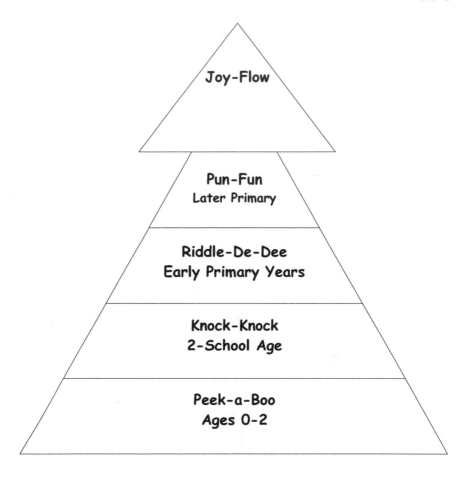

Stages of Humor Development

Figure 2-2.

Peek-a-Boo (Birth to Two Years)

Parents work very hard to elicit that first smile from their newborn. My daughter Rachael and her husband, Jason, recently had their first daughter, Katie. From the moment she was born they have cooed, smiled, and talked to her. When she smiles, they respond with great enthusiasm. They were ecstatic about capturing her first outburst of laughter on video in her response to Jason acting silly with a toy elephant. Katie's humor journey has begun.

Babies carefully observe their caregivers and intently respond to smiles with mirroring smiles and mimicking laughter. The process of reading the faces of others initiates social development and provides a basis for bonding between caregivers and the child. Around five or six months, babies recognize parents/caregivers and will frown or cry when strangers approach.

The game of peek-a-boo assures the child that what disappears will reappear. This game helps children understand that their caregiver will return. The initial fear of loss is replaced with surprised relief which eventually results in laughter. This laughter is appreciated by adults and the game is frequently repeated. My granddaughter Mimi at age ten months found great delight in pulling the diaper off of her mother's face in a reverse game of peek-a-boo.

Adults engage infants in numerous games that provide the basic skills for the "reading" of emotions. Silly noises, hiding objects, repetition of nonsense sounds, and roughhousing all elicit laughter while forming the trusted relationships necessary for humor development. These fun games also contribute to the foundation of a strong attachment between parent and child.

Around the age of one year, incongruent behavior on the part of a caregiver (such as pretending to eat the child's cracker) will evoke laughter (Ziv, 1984). Repetition of silly behaviors will amuse children of this age, while rhythm and rhyme engage their sensory abilities.

When my twin grandsons were twenty-two months old, one of their favorite songs was "Twinkle Twinkle, Little Star." While singing with them in the car, I changed the word *star* to their names (Benjamin and Tyler) and then a variety of other names. They kept saying, "No Grandma, star!". I finally sang it the right way and Ben said "No Grandma—Tyler!" followed by laughter. He obviously was able to understand and replicate the surprise change pattern or "joke."

Chasing games and physical contact play are important aspects of this stage. At eighteen months, my granddaughters Mimi and Christine were laughing and coming back for more when this grandma would say: "I'm going to get you!" followed by a chase around the dining room table.

The peek-a-boo stage builds the relational foundation of trust and hope necessary for emotional intelligence and for building infant attachment to a primary caregiver. It also supports the ability of the toddler to understand disruption in normal patterns of human behavior so they can transition to the knock-knock phase.

Jest for Fun

Have students/teachers bring in their baby pictures. Have a contest to identify who is who. Write about physical and emotional characteristics in infancy.

Knock-Knock (Two Years to School Age)

At age two-and-a-half Samuel declared that his grandma was sure silly when she sang and exaggerated the movements to several songs. Of course, Samuel is right, as I love watching the response of my grandchildren to my dorky behavior. Pretend behaviors, exaggeration of reality, and imagination emerge in this stage of humor development. Within Piaget's preoperational stage emerges the capacity for children to appreciate fantasy creatures and to employ their own imagination to create silly stories and drawings. Dramatic play begins with children imitating adult behavior. They use their imagination to pretend, often laughing at their own ingenuity.

After we made cookies, my twenty-three-month-old grandson, Andrew, was helping me to wipe up the crumbs on the floor. He wiped the top of my feet and looked up at me with a smile. When I acknowledged his silly humor by laughing, he laughed heartily, obviously happy that I "got his joke." He repeated this silly pattern several times, always looking to be sure I appreciated his humor. Bathroom humor emerges at this stage and reflects the concerns that children have with their own bodily functions. Taboo words and laughter about body parts are common in early childhood. Jokes about elimination and sexual ideas are often accompanied with giggles. Numerous creative books have been written on these topics.

"Know why Miss Tomato turned red? Because she saw Mr. Green Pea!" It is intriguing to note the use of humor in children's literature. Word play and repetition are important in the knock-knock stage of humor development. Three- to five-year-olds begin to find humor in things that appear incongruent, such as an elephant washing a car. Dr. Seuss has become a timeless example of the combination of rhythm, rhyme, ridiculous characters, and imaginative storylines that appeal to children of all ages. Media exposure has made Big Bird and Cookie Monster, as well as Barney and Elmo common household names. Many movies today have a parallel humor track appealing to the different cognition levels of both children and adults. *Finding Nemo*, *Shrek*, and *Antz* delight audiences of all ages.

Emerging social relationships start to mirror group laughter and humor. *Group glee* is a wave of laughter that emerges from a group of playing children. One reason I loved teaching kindergarten children is that they found humor in most situations and easily shared the laughter. Children take pleasure in trying to fool adults with "knock-knock jokes" and silly riddles. Parents who take the time to nurture this stage are encouraging the capacity for the future divergent thinking required for innovative problem solving and creativity. Encouraging the use of nonsense words, word plays, and rhyme supports the acquisition of the foundational tools necessary for humor skills.

Knock-knock jokes are actually a fairly advanced skill since there are five steps in the process:

1. The originator says: "Knock-knock."
2. The recipient says: "Who's there?"
3. The originator responds, usually with a first name.
4. The recipient asks for clarification by saying the name plus "Who?"
5. The punch line is a deliberate addition to the word set-up in the third response. This is usually in the format of a last name and linked to the first name so that the first name has a different meaning.

🔳 Jest for Fun 🔳

Have a "knock-knock joke" day. Everyone brings their favorite one and shares with the class.

Knock-knock.
Who's there?
Dewey.
Dewey who?
Dewey like knock-knock jokes?

This format is a good basis for children beginning to understand that words can have two meanings. Unfortunately for parents and teachers of children at this stage, these jokes can get pretty tedious.

Riddle-De-Dee (Early Primary Years)

Parents and educators have a significant role in modeling humor and providing strategies to build relationships. "Children with the ability to use humor skills in social interactions were found to be chosen for social activities more often than children with less developed skills" (McGhee, 2002a).

The comprehension of verbal irony seems to emerge between five and six years of age. Jokes, riddles, and clowns begin to be appreciated by children. Practicing jokes and repeating riddles are valuable components in this stage of humor development. Teachers can generate excitement for reading through joke and riddle books, especially for those students who might not be too enthusiastic about other kinds of literature. Since children are drawn to these books, many educators use them to promote vocabulary development, encourage creativity, and improve reading skills. Comic books, funny stories, and cartoons embedded in the curriculum contribute to the fun of learning. A great resource for children on how to create riddles is *Stumble Bees and Pelephones* (McGhee 2002a). McGhee says that humor is really a form of intellectual play. Playing with ideas forms the foundation of creative thinking.

"My dog can lick anyone.

 Jest for Fun

Use the web as a resource for riddles that correlate to your lesson planning. Incorporate into testing, activities, and homework. Give extra credit to students who create riddles that reflect the lesson plan.

Pun-Fun (Later Primary Years, Grades 4–8)

Children at this stage are moving toward increased understanding of the subtle differences in language and their more fully developed language skills accelerate their humor appreciation. Word play, language variations, and the magic of the English language become a magnet that will captivate children during grades 4–8. This is the period where the students will be able to detect and enjoy a language twist at the end of a story. They will also be able to understand a subtle variance in word selection and therefore "get the joke." Puns and satire are beginning to be understood by students and there are initial attempts to invent their own pun-fun.

The ability to discern the variances in language is essential for humor development. Ziv, in his book *Personality and a Sense of Humor* (1984), wrote that in order to enjoy humor, a person must understand the nuances of the language. Understanding the nature of humor development can be invaluable for both teachers of special education and for teachers of talented students. Special education teachers find that using jokes and riddles can assist in the language and reading skill development of their students. And since a sense of humor is an indicator of language comprehension, it is often one of the characteristics for identifying linguistically talented students.

The pun-fun stage also requires the capacity to perceive differences between feelings of joy, surprise, silliness, happiness, and sarcasm, all necessary elements for humor development. The emotional growth of the child is an important factor in appreciating and learning to use humor at this stage. This can have negative as well as positive results. Since slapstick humor and laughing at the mistakes of others are commonly experienced within the social structure of these grades, teachers need to be prepared to share positive humor techniques with their students. It's important for students to have positive role models for humor practice.

The middle years initiate the emergence of puberty with jokes about sex and aggressive behavior. Adolescents experience anxiety about the changes they are experiencing physically and this sexual humor can provide relief from the stress of puberty. As with the bathroom humor of earlier ages, physical changes evoke challenges for preteens, who resort to laughing with others as a coping device. Note: some folks never outgrow the bathroom/sexual humor stages.

Puns emerge from the clever massaging of the English language, usually evoking groans from listeners. These groans act as fertilizer for the pun-nuts, as it definitely encourages them to expand their punning.

Groups of punsters can be dangerous. They build on each other and delight in how far they can string out a punny. Many students love using puns related to the lesson. Ask them to think of puns on the topic of the day. A lesson on the importance of calcium and the consumption of milk can lead to puns on the good *moo*d that milk provides and how it is *udder*ly delicious. Whether it is creating puns, practicing the rhymes of Dr. Seuss, or doing a comparative analysis of Shakespeare's tragedies and comedies, there is a tremendous opportunity to nurture humor at this stage.

A word about class clowns—the entertainers trying to get the entire class to laugh. There is no doubt about the havoc that class clowns can bring to a classroom. Even though the ability to create group laughter is a valued life skill, we usually negate and even punish initial attempts of these risk-taking youngsters in schools. These children can shine if encouraged to use their humor to strengthen social bonds. Numerous comedians admit to starting their careers in school as class clowns. Fortunately they had teachers who provided the solid ground necessary for these nuts to succeed in the world of comedy. Chapter 6 provides additional resources for growing these nuts and nurturing their creativity.

"A good time to keep your mouth shut is when you are in deep water."

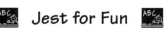

Jest for Fun

Sponsor "A Pun Day Fun Day." Use your lesson for the day as the theme. Incorporate puns into the assessments.

Joy-Flow (Maturation of Humor Style, High School to Adult)

We have mentioned the ultimate or peak experience as identified by Maslow and described by Mihaly Csikszentmihalyi as a flow or a spiritual experience (Csikszentmihalyi, 1997). Humergy is extraordinary optimism and a passionate energy for life combined with a gentle understanding of others. It describes the energy that radiates the optimistic joy of our inner spirit, reflects our unique personality, and nourishes a healthy mind/body balance. Joy-flow is the degree to which we have accomplished optimal growth and self-discovery. This peak experience exemplifies the capacity to view challenges with optimistic amusement. A heightened state of positive emotionality defines the fun-finder's peak experience. For many, joy-flow is a spiritual journey.

Becoming aware of our sense of humor provides an opportunity to expand our humor energy through humor practice. This experience of flow and energy will create a natural euphoric high. I invite you to take this opportunity to review the humor strength reflections found in appendix 4: Sense of Humor Reflections to reflect on what types of humor produce a joy-flow in you.

Once there is an understanding of the emotional self, it transcends to an understanding of others. Humergy encourages listening and honoring feelings, both of self and of others. It is an understanding that anger often mirrors feelings of fear. The experience of humergy in groups encourages trusted relationships providing mutual support for facing life challenges.

Joy-flow also is evident within groups. Visualize a classroom of laughing students filled with excitement, where each school day offers opportunities for brain-compatible learning facilitated by passionately optimistic teachers. Picture a school office with a laughing staff energized by the prospect of providing a fun-filled parent program that evening and excited about the challenges of the upcoming referendum.

Humergy is the energy that radiates the humorous optimism of our inner spirit. It is the positive emotionality that creates a healthy mind/body balance. It is observed in students, teachers, and administrators who are passionate about learning, ecstatic about attending a school that supports positive emotionality, and where fun is an integral part of the learning experience. This joy-flow state and the possible connections to learning provide significant opportunities for further study.

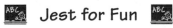

Jest for Fun

Try swinging. Go to your nearest park and get on a swing. It is a lot of fun and great exercise. Casually tell your colleagues that you are a "real" swinger!

UNIVERSAL HUMOR ELEMENTS

Woven through these developmental stages are several elements that have a profound impact on the development of humor beings. These cut across the temperament and developmental aspects of humor and are the emotional components of trust, hope, optimism, and loving relationships. In our efforts to learn about humor we will review in depth the emerging research about the significant impact emotions have on learning in chapter 3. However there is a need to mention a few of the emotional indicators that are lifelong partners of humor development and practice.

Trust. Fun and laughter are indicators of a high level of trust within a healthy organization.

Hope. Humor is the sign of optimism within individuals and organizations. Humor expresses the hope that we can survive tragedy, difficulty, and change and not only survive but thrive.

Optimism. Depression and pessimism are often linked. The energy of humor is a reflection of an optimistic spirit.

Love. When looking for a mate, the number one characteristic mentioned as necessary is a sense of humor. Humor is the universal bond for building relationships and reflects our love for others.

Finding and nourishing the nut within you is a lifelong adventure. The energy that comes from humor supports our ability to be optimistic, to have trust and hope, and to experience loving relationships.

> "Even a blind squirrel finds a nut once in awhile."

SUMMARY

This chapter examines the impact of temperament on our development and the power of play in brain growth. We are born with a temperament that impacts our humor development and our environment nurtures the growth of our sense of humor. There are five defined stages of humor development:

1. Peek-a-boo, ages zero to two
2. Knock-knock, ages two to school age
3. Riddle-de-dee, early primary years
4. Pun-fun, later primary years
5. Joy-flow, maturation of humor style, high school to adult

Each stage has opportunities for enhancing learning and it is important for educators to have an awareness of the developmental characteristics of each stage. Each infant's brain contains a unique blueprint for humor maturation. Recognition of universal patterns of humor development provides the foundation for cultivating individual growth through specific jokes and humorous techniques for that particular phase.

Play is an integral part of brain growth and of humor development. Play provides powerful practice opportunities for cognitive development. However, in this age of accountability, schools reduce free play as structured test-driven activities consume more and more time. Playfulness is deemed acceptable only in controlled situations and with certain rituals that permit the expression of silliness, fun, and wild laughter. Play necessitates a level of risk taking rarely tolerated as acceptable behavior in most groups. Yet many organizations are recognizing the importance of play in generating creativity, productivity, and employee well-being. A sign of a healthy school environment is one that is filled with fun and laughter. Humor is an indicator of a high level of trust within a culture. Humor is reflected in the universal positive elements of trust, hope, optimism, and love.

Powerful Practice—Strategies for School Leaders

☺ Use humor as an intentional, attentional tool.
☺ Generate discussion of these definitions among the staff. Divide staff into several or all of these groups. Have them design activities based on their topic:
  ☺ Practicing Play: The Original Discovery Method of Learning
  ☺ The Art of Fun: The Real Definition of Engaged Learning
  ☺ Mindful Mischief: Minimize Misbehaviors with Mirth
  ☺ Class Clowns: Honoring and Developing Student Humor
  ☺ Funny Papers: Writing with Humor and Cartooning
  ☺ Emotion Detector: A Skill Used to Understand the Emotions of Self and Others
☺ Start staff meetings honoring the person who has created the most laughter in the building that week. Have a traveling "Oscar" trophy.

☺ Have a "lettuce entertains you" salad luncheon for institute day. Take pictures of staff with a "make over" as clowns. Let different groups create games, activities, and opportunities for fun.

☺ Sponsor a "Letterman top ten list" for some of the problems or situations in the school or district (for example: "The top ten reasons why school board meetings are fun to attend" or "The top ten reasons for being the first person to be in the building in the morning").

☺ Start a jokers club. Invite all interested to join in sharing jokes, stories, and cartoons. Meet weekly, beginning with a half hour time slot. This could be over the lunch hour, before, or after school. Use a deck of cards to begin the session. The person who draws the "joker" first gets to begin the session.

Study Group Focus

☺ Observe the humor development of the students in your classroom.

☺ Brainstorm with your colleagues some ways to optimize student learning.

☺ Create a plan to increase the humor resources in the library based on current student development needs.

☺ Research current levels of play and free choice in your school environment.

☺ Do a climate survey of students and staff before implementation of a focused effort to increase play time for students and staff. After a year of implementation do a follow-up survey. Note any change in climate, test scores, parent satisfaction, etc.

☺ Study the current status of play time for students and staff including recess, lunch, staff breaks, retreats, etc. Share your findings with students and staff.

☺ Analyze the play data and brainstorm ways to increase the amount of free play and choice for students and staff.

Café Conversations

☺ Discuss the play research found in this chapter. Expand the discussion to include the views of early childhood educators and high school colleagues. Is there a difference in the way play is considered as a part of the curriculum?

☺ What is creative thinking? After coming to shared agreement, explore the various ways that educators encourage students' creativity.

☺ What are the benefits and challenges of class clowns? List ways that teachers can take advantage of the gifts of class clowns.

"Birthdays are good for you. The more you have, the longer you live."

Chapter 3

EXAMINING BRAIN RESEARCH AND HUMOR

Mouse Droppings

"It has recently been discovered that research causes cancer in rats."

Pioneering research continues to unravel ways in which humor and learning are linked. Two kinds of mice are providing us with increasingly detailed information about the role of the emotions in the learning process. These mouse droppings provide powerful incentives for us to take a fresh look at humor as a significant factor in the learning process.

Laboratory mice. Those little critters and their researchers persist in providing us data about the links between the emotions, learning, and humor.

Computer mouse. Another type of mouse manipulation is found in the use of computerized imaging. The ability to observe brain activity has accelerated our understanding of cognitive research. Cognitive neuroscience continues to address how brain biology addresses the emotions and learning.

MRI technology provides us with some mesmerizing data on what humor looks like in the brain. Machines are able to measure variations in chemical composition, blood flow, and electromagnetic fields. This technology has dramatically advanced the ability of brain scientists to provide clinical applications. The research on humor shows that the chemical reactions that occur while we laugh are complex, which affirms that what we know about humor and cognition is primitive at best. The quest for knowledge linking the positive emotions and learning can be compared to a mouse in a maze looking for the cheesy humor. It will be a long journey!

Brain research has provided the foundation for my thinking about humor. Numerous books are listed in the bibliography, but *Becoming a Wiz at Brain-Based Teaching* (Sprenger 2002) and *Brain Matters, Translating Research into Classroom Practice* (Wolfe, 2001) are excellent resources for teachers wanting to incorporate brain research into their practice. *Blueprint for Student Success* (Jones, 2003) and *A Biological Brain in a Cultural Classroom* (Sylwester, 2003) are also exceptional resources.

Funny, isn't it? Humor has not even been on the radar screen of most educational researchers. Following the trail of mouse droppings has been a pioneering adventure. However, there are several pellets that make the case for using positive humor to maximize learning (see figure 3-1). This

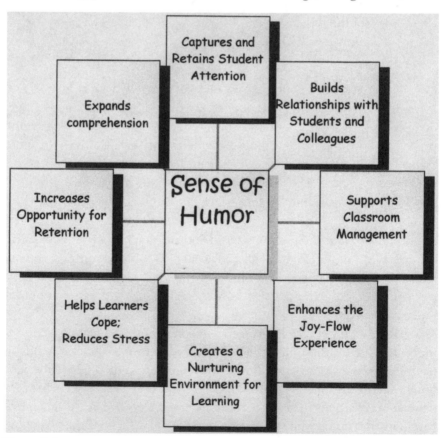

Figure 3-1.

chapter will examine the research on the role of emotions in fear, stress, and depression. I will then look at how humor can:

☺ Capture and retain student attention
☺ Expand student comprehension
☺ Increase the opportunity for memory retention
☺ Build relationships with students and colleagues
☺ Create a nurturing environment for learning
☺ Support classroom management
☺ Help people cope
☺ Enhance the joyful craft of teaching and learning

THE EMOTIONS AND HUMOR

An overview of the research confirms that humor is a complex process involving our emotional being. The research on emotions provides the essential foundation necessary for humor studies. Emotion is an unconscious arousal system that helps to alert us to potential dangers as well as opportunities. The emotions identify the dynamics of challenge and activate the problem-solving systems to respond. Almost everything we do begins with the complex processing system of emotion (Sylwester, 2005).

Learning must go through our emotional filter and our memories are composed of experiences that are linked to emotions. Thus, emotional memory is a critical component for the learning process. These emotions are either positively or negatively linked. As educators, what do we want our students to feel? What do we want to feel?

 Jest for Fun

Before reading this next section, think about three of your most powerful memories of school. Why do you remember them? What emotions were tied to these memories?

We know from our friend the imaging mouse that much of the activity of humor occurs in the frontal lobes of the brain. The frontal lobes are the problem-solving, decision-making, action-initiating, paired lobes in the front part of the cerebral cortex (Sylwester, 2005). The frontal lobes recognize incongruities or discrepancies between the predicted developments and what actually occurs. All of our senses are designed to go on high alert when observing unusual patterns in our field of vision because our stress-driven reflective response system is designed to detect anything that might harm us. If what occurs is what is expected, we don't really take notice. If what occurs is unexpected and negative (danger), and we lack the resources to respond effectively, a pessimistic state emerges—becoming fearful, pessimistic, angry, etc. Conversely, if what occurs is unexpected and positive (opportunity) and we have the resources to respond effectively, we move into a state of joy—becoming happy, optimistic, etc. Our memory is strongly linked to positive or negative emotions.

The emotions are a critical force in the learning process. According to Antonio R. Damasio, "emotion is a very adaptive form of physiological response, and it regulates our lives." He states that emotion is part of the reasoning and decision-making process and is critical to learning and memory. Our very survival system depends upon the emotions as part of our regulatory system (Damasio, 1999). Sylwester (1995) states that "emotions drive attention, attention drives learning." Candice Pert (1997), a pioneer in cellular research, hypothesizes that emotions exist in every cell of the body. She actually started investigating neuropeptides when she read Norman Cousin's work *Anatomy of an Illness* (1979). Her research explores the brain chemicals of mood and behavior and how they communicate with the immune system and she was interested in his theory that endorphins are the key to the healing power of laughter. Her theory is that our emotions exist in every cell in our body and not just in our brains; thus, when we have a strong emotion, we feel it in our entire body. Although there is some controversy about this theory, there is no doubt that our emotions play a vital role in attention, memory, and learning.

If we were a mouse in the corner of a school building, what emotions would we observe among teachers and students? Joy or fear? Since fear can and does immediately activate the reflective response system of our brain, it has long been used to manipulate teacher behavior and student learning. This controlling tactic is evident in our school systems. The fear of teacher evaluations, of parent confrontations, of bad grades, the fear of being sent to the principal's office, and the fear of not getting into college are widespread fear-based factors. Educators and students must frequently navigate the emotional land mine of fear-based emotions in our schools. We need to take a close look at the emotion of fear in order to better understand humor.

Fear is our most powerful emotion. It has the primary purpose of protecting us from harm. We are programmed to pay attention to our fears because this emotion alerts us if our safety is threatened. Fear has been the focus of considerable cognitive research. Imaging technology makes it relatively easy to locate fear in the amygdala and hippocampus regions of the brain. Fear signals *danger*. Fear immediately alerts us to pay attention.

While this fear is critical to our survival, it is tempting to use this emotional reaction to control the actions of others. Let's look at some of the research on stress in order to appreciate the subsequent research on humor and fun.

STRESS AND LEARNING

Excess fear causes stress. There is mounting scientific evidence that suggests that excess stress has an adverse impact on learning. Yet, according to many teachers, we are exposing our children to stress at escalating rates. There has been increased high-stakes testing in our schools and many districts have implemented paper and pencil testing for students as young as four and five years old. There has been an increasing pressure to focus on what is tested (reading and math) at the expense of the arts, physical education, and play. Grades are considered extremely important and actually drive most students' learning instead of the desire to learn.

A look at some of the research heightens our awareness of the possible dangers that excess stress creates for our students. Although there are no firm conclusions, here are some of the recent theories on the relationship between stress, depression, memory, and learning.

An impoverished and stressful childhood may diminish learning by having a negative impact on the medial temporal memory of a child. Prenatal stress and the stress that comes from living in poverty have been found to have a negative impact on neurological development and subsequent ability to learn (Farah, 2005).

Excess fear might lead to actual memory loss. Robert Sapolsky conducted a fascinating study examining the brains of World War II veterans who had survived intense trauma during the war. He found that the hippocampus of these men was usually smaller than nonveterans in the same age category. He noted an actual loss of part of the hippocampus in these veterans as well as a resulting memory loss (Sapolsky, 1999). Current studies corroborate this relationship between excess stress, damage to the hippocampus, and subsequent memory loss, but no firm conclusions can be made yet.

Overuse or misuse of the reflexive response system can escalate simple anger and assertiveness into reflexive physical aggression. Some students constantly live in an insecure fearful environment, producing a learned helplessness response (Sylwester, 2005). Often students just give up when they feel they have no control over their environment. "A reflexive stress response occurs unconsciously, and so reduces our ability to create factual memories" (Sylwester, 2005).

> "Before giving anyone a piece of your mind, be sure you have enough to spare."

DEPRESSION

Students who are prone to depression may secrete more cortisol during a stressful time. There may also be decreased prefrontal cortex activity, causing moody and negative behavior. Depressed students have trouble concentrating. Symptoms of depression also include deteriorating schoolwork, truancy, verbal outbursts, and social rejection (Sylwester, 2005).

Depression should not be overlooked when it comes to its impact on teaching and learning. "It is not possible to explain either the disease or its treatment based solely on levels of neurotransmitters," says neurobiologist Ronald Duman (1999).

> There is evidence that indicates that recurrent depression is in fact a neurodegenerative disorder, disrupting the structure and function of brain cells—destroying nerve cell connections, even killing certain brain cells, and precipitating cognitive decline. At the very least, depression sets up neural roadblocks to the processing of information and keeps us from adaptively responding to whatever challenges life throws our way. (Estroff Marano, 1999)

HIGH-STAKES TESTING

There have not been enough studies to clearly address this issue; however, some of the research indicates a correlation between stress and high-stakes testing. Researchers at Arizona State University conducted a fairly large study on standardized testing and reported that high-stakes testing can induce physiologically damaging stress. Teachers interviewed reported increased levels of stress as a result of the testing process, including extreme frustration and exhaustion. An in-depth examination of elementary schools in Arizona found that external (i.e., state- and district-mandated) high-stakes testing often resulted in negative effects in the classroom (Wright 2002).

MAXIMIZING LEARNING WITH HUMOR

Our brain is wired to notice unusual movement and abnormal activity. This information is filtered by the reflexive response system of the brain and alerts us to possible danger. This same system also feels relief if the danger is nonexistent. This feeling of relief is often what triggers humor. So humor is a tool that can be used by the reflexive response center of the brain that monitors our environment for fear. When the brain discovers there is no danger, the surprise brings relief that often generates laughter and humor. Humor thus can provide the tools needed to cope with fear and stress.

As promised, we will look at how humor enhances learning. I have grouped the first three humor learning elements within the metaphor of using humor as a hook, line, and sinker for memory and learning. These are described as tools that can fill the "educator's tackle box" (see figure 3-2):

The Hook: Capture and Retain Student Attention
The Line: Expand Student Comprehension
The Sinker: Increase the Opportunity for Memory Retention

How do you activate the hook, line, and sinker tools in your tackle box? *Hook 'em* with humor. Cast in the *line* of practice and repetition, and *sink* it in the long-term memory with feedback and reflection.

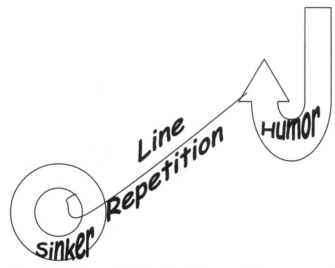

Figure 3-2.   Your tackle box: hook, line, and sinker

The process described in this metaphor involves a purposeful and determined use of humor for the purpose of memory retention. Humor has the power to capture attention (hook), manipulate this information in the working memory (line), and become a part of our automatic response system (sinker).

The Hook

The brain is hardwired to familiar patterns. The way we drive or the way we approach solving a math problem becomes routine. Over time our repetitious daily activity follows established habits of behavior. As previously mentioned, fear protects us from danger. In order to do this, the brain is alerted to a pattern disruption or any surprise element. As a protective device when we see something out of the ordinary—we notice. This surprise component is what provides the opportunity for teachers to effectively use humor because humor usually contains an element of surprise.

Surprise defies the brain's predictions and expectations. When someone acts out of the ordinary, when something unusual happens, our brain pays attention. It is often recommended in implementing differentiation strategies that teachers change state every ten to fifteen minutes to "wake up" the attentional center of the brain. This change of state assists the students who may no longer be paying attention. A humor hook is perfect bait for the educator's tackle box.

The Line

The hook is followed with a line, a direct connection that links past experiences with the new information. The emotional memory is strong. Humor can be used to activate the brain by linking the emotional context of humor, thus finding the information that we want to remember. We can provide this humor context through repetition and practice. These are the critical components in creating strong lines or neural pathways to the long-term memory. Neurons that fire together, wire together. Practice and repetition condition our brains and form pathways that will become "hardwired." These neural connections streamline the learning process. Learning is quicker, more automatic, and more efficient when pathways in the brain are frequently traveled.

The more humor that is interjected into student practice (instead of boring rote stuff), the more likely it is students will want to repeat the information and strengthen the neural pathway. A strong line is dependent on frequent usage. If it's fun, it will be practiced.

The Sinker

Several authors of the brain-based literature detail strategies for using feedback and reflection as tools for sinking the information into long-term memory and ensuring recall (Jones, 2003). Humor can be used by the teacher to assist in the feedback loop of assessment. Again, the more humor links (emotional memory) provided for the brain, the better chance there will be for recalling information. Reflection is the remaining chance to use humor and can be a powerful tool for subsequent memory recall. Other powerful sinker techniques are summary, assessment, and authentic assessment, (performing a real life task).

So humor has the power to capture attention (hook). If you manipulate this information through practice and repetition in the working memory (line), it becomes a part of our automatic response system (sinker) with feedback and reflection. The frequency of humor implemented at any of these points improves the probability that the emotional memory will be found and the student will remember the information.

Many teachers informally use humor as an integral part of teaching students for memory retention and recall. However, what I am suggesting here is a *purposeful use of humor* applied to what we already know from cognitive research. There are numerous examples of hook, line, and sinker techniques included in chapter 6.

An example of using humor hook, line, and sinker can be found in the popular *Schoolhouse Rock* cartoons, a commercial advertising venture by David McCall. He noticed that his son was having trouble with remembering the multiplication tables; however, he had no trouble remembering the lyrics to many rock songs. So McCall decided to try the music and rhyme his son already enjoyed as a way to teach these facts. The first song created was "Three Is a Magic Number," by Bob Dorough. It became so popular that subsequent episodes were added for other content areas, including grammar and science. This series is an example of hooking kids with cartoons and providing the line with practice and repetition. Teachers can sink the information through feedback by asking students what they remember from the video. Students can repeat and even sing the information as a way to reflect on their learning. My granddaughter Emma spent our last car trip singing the ABC song. I would venture a guess that most of us "sing" that song when asked to recite the alphabet.

Some resources that integrate humor and learning are available, but further exploration is needed on ways that humor resources can maximize student learning.

"A mouse does not rely on just one hole."—Plautus

HUMOR BUILDS RELATIONSHIPS
WITH FRIENDS AND COLLEAGUES

Developing positive relationships with students and colleagues is one of the greatest benefits of humor. Laughter is a visible sign of humor in action and reflects the social side of humor.

Why do we laugh? When do we laugh? What connection does laughter have to humor? Robert Provine, in his book *Laughter, a Scientific In-*

vestigation (2000), makes it clear that it is difficult to research humor because of the variety of definitions and vague terminology. However, laughter is observable and he says, "because laughter is unplanned and uncensored, it is a powerful probe into social relationships."

While laughter is generally thought to be an expression of humor or comedy, it is definitely observed most often during social interactions with others and does not necessarily result from jokes or funny stories. Provine uses the term *sidewalk science*, which he says is a low-tech approach to brain and behavior research based on everyday experience. His observations of human laugher and an analysis of subsequent recorded conversations are the basis for his interpretation that laughter can be considered a distinct vocalization that usually occurs during positive social interactions (Provine, 2000).

Philosopher John Morreall speculates that human laughter may have its biological origins as a shared expression of relief at the ending of danger. The relaxation we feel after laughing may help inhibit the fight-or-flight response, making laughter a behavioral sign of trust in one's companions.

> Laughter is a part of human behavior regulated by the brain. It helps humans clarify their intentions in social interaction and provides an emotional context to our conversations. Laughter is used as a signal for being part of a group—it signals acceptance and positive interactions. Laughter is sometimes contagious and the laughter of one person can provoke laughter from others. This may account for the popularity of laugh tracks in situation comedy television shows. Imaging studies reveal that the limbic system is involved in laughter. The limbic system is a primitive part of the brain that is involved in emotions and helps us with basic functions necessary for survival. Two structures in the limbic system are involved in producing laughter: the amygdala and the hippocampus. (Morreall, 1997)

The Rotman Research Institute at the University of Toronto released the first study to show that the frontal lobe plays a prominent role in our ability to appreciate humor. The study, led by Prathiba Shammi, measured responses to jokes and cartoons. Half of the group had injury to the prefrontal lobes caused by stroke, tumor, or surgical removal. The responses of this group were compared to a control group similar in age, gender, and education. The study found that damage to the right anterior frontal lobe was disruptive to the ability to appreciate jokes and cartoons (Shammi, 1999).

Peter Derks conducted a study of laughter using electrodes attached to the brain. The electricity observed in the entire cerebral cortex indicated that most of the brain is actively engaged during laughter. Laughter can be just a simple physical response to the nonhumorous stimulus of tickling, while positive social interactions usually evoke a smile, laugh, or chuckle and can be thought of as eliciting the laughter response (1997).

There have been several studies of the benefits of laughter. Some research indicates that laughter increases adrenaline, oxygen flow, and pulse rate. After laughter, many people report feeling more relaxed and calm. Laughter can be observed in relationships with another person or with several others. The relatively new research on mirror neurons suggests that our brain has a basic mirroring response to emotional actions.

> When parents conceive a child, their combined genetic information provides the developing embryo with the necessary bodybuilding directions—such as gender identity, nose placement, and skin color. After the child is born, parents and others must provide cultural information about how to live in our complex social environment. They provide this mentoring through language and our brain's remarkable recently discovered mirror neuron system.
>
> The renowned neuroscientist V. S. Ramachandran suggested at the turn of the 21st century that the discovery of mirror neurons might provide the same powerful unifying framework for our understanding of teaching and learning that the 1953 discovery of DNA did for our understanding of genetics. Recent developments suggest that his prediction might be correct.
>
> He goes on to say, "When we observe someone yawn, it activates our brain's yawning system. Adults typically override the tendency and stifle the yawn—but if we stick out our tongue at an infant who is only a few hours old, it's probable that she will immediately reciprocate, even though she had never before stuck out her tongue (or even had any conscious awareness of her tongue). Her observation of our behavior will automatically activate the mirror neurons that regulate her tongue movements. Since she has a zillion movements to learn and therefore no reason to stifle the action, her mirror neurons will activate the motor neurons that project her tongue. Similarly, smile and she'll smile. Clap your hands and she'll clap her hands. It's like monkey see, monkey do in childhood." (Sylwester, 2006)

Research on mirror neurons as related to humor and laughter will be fascinating to observe. We do know that laughter is contagious. When someone laughs, even if the situation is not funny, we will often join the laughter. How do the mirror neurons figure into this? As humor pioneers, we can only imagine what future research will reveal.

> "All creatures must learn to coexist. That's why the brown bear and the field mouse can share their lives in harmony. Of course, they can't mate or the mice would explode."
>
> —Betty White

HUMOR CREATES A NURTURING ENVIRONMENT FOR LEARNING

One of my favorite "mouse droppings" involves the impact of different cage environments on rats. (See figure 3-3.) Could positive experiences change the actual physical structure of the brain? Rats were put in three different environments. The first rats were loners raised in dark isolation with only food and water. The second set was raised with other rats in a small but social group. The third group of rats was treated to a condition called environmental complexity. These fortunate rats lived in colonies of twelve with toys and frequent stimulation from the scientists. These lucky rats did indeed have larger brain mass and performed better on problem-solving maze tasks. A subsequent study (Volkmar & Greenough, 1972) found that the brains of rats in the wild had the most neural connections, which might lead us to ask if our schools are just cages with toys and friends!

Educators have long known an enriched environment contributes to better performance in school and a better chance of success in life (Diamond & Hopson, 1998). Parents are a child's first educators and most children do not come with instructions—at least mine didn't. Children come to school with a wide range of backgrounds and previous experiences, which have an enormous impact on student learning.

Since our personalities emerge from our genetics and our emotionally stored memories (LeDeux, 2002), it seems probable that our humor identity comes from the experiences of joy, laughter, and fun stored in

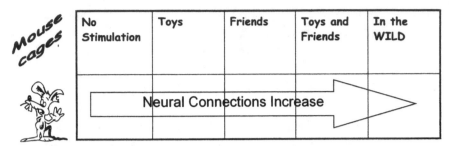

Mouse cages	No Stimulation	Toys	Friends	Toys and Friends	In the WILD
	Neural Connections Increase				

Figure 3-3.

our memories and from the temperament that we inherited. This is the nature/nurture theory explored in chapter 2. The more humor experiences an individual has, the better the chance that humor will benefit the learning process.

A positive emotional relationship with significant adults provides the emotional groundwork for the neurological development of a child from birth (Siegel, 1999). When a child enters preschool, the emotional response system is fairly well developed. There are children who are unable to respond appropriately in a school environment because they do not have the emotional tools necessary. We notice the sad and angry kids, we usually notice the kids who are depressed, and we always notice the kids who act out. We often explore the causes of "dysfunction" and try to provide appropriate services.

Our schools have a unique opportunity to provide a "wild rat experience" toward maximizing learning for all of our children. This learning is active, engaging, and absorbing for students. Unfortunately, many of our children are in deprived school environments, like the second or even the first group of rats. A sit-and-get lectured style school environment may be compared to the cage that offers no toys or little stimulation for the students. (Refer to figure 3-3.)

Kids and adults can learn to route the neural pathways in their brains toward positive response patterns. Exploring ways for kids to focus on their positive emotions can be a challenge. Hey, it's also a challenge for most of us as adults. It begins with the premise that learning is fun. Any worthwhile work that actively engages the mind and provides excitement and challenge can be identified as fun. If children are having fun, their emotional state will be one of positive anticipation.

They will be eager to absorb the hook, line, and sinker of humor-filled learning (see appendix 1).

HUMOR SUPPORTS CLASSROOM MANAGEMENT

"Won't I lose class control if I use humor?" This question has been often been raised by teachers. There is a perception that students who are laughing and having fun are out of control. Humor guidelines (see impact vs. intent in chapter 4) might be reviewed with older students who have not previously been encouraged to express their energy and joy. There is a euphoric high experienced by students when they have successfully gotten the class to laugh or when they find humor in learning. This is humergy in action.

The emotional state of the child cannot be overlooked. If a child comes to school in an angry mood, most teachers try to dissolve the anger, knowing angry kids will not be ready to learn. Teachers also have the opportunity to teach children the internal skill of being able to change their own fearful/angry pattern of response to one of hope and optimism, open to the possibility of humor and joy.

Fourth graders enrolled in a program called Urban Improv Workshops showed less aggression and were more engaged in class, according to an article in the *Christian Science Monitor* (Teicher, 2005). This Boston research study conducted by the Trauma Center of the Massachusetts Mental Health Institute compared a control group with the group that used humor and improv workshops to decrease the aggressive behavior. The participant group showed more cooperation, self-control, and engagement in class than the control group. This was a limited study that needs further peer review but provides an initial step in this type of research.

Have you noticed? There are the experienced teachers who have the ability to anticipate disruptive behavior *before* it happens. These truly gifted teachers often use humor to deter misbehavior while continuing to let that same student know they are cared for. Kidding is a successful strategy that has long been used by teachers who especially love the kids who live on the edge of trouble. Sylwester (2005) defines this kidding as always showing love and respect for the person, even though the actual words may be interpreted as negative. This class management technique is a phenomenon that has been primarily unnoticed. Novice teachers could benefit from observation of teachers who are gifted "kidders." This is another opportunity for additional mouse droppings research.

Fun and laughter must be in the teacher's tackle box as well. If students observe teachers using humor as an automatic response to the unexpected, they will notice that there is an alternative emotional response to life's difficulties. Teachers can model the desired humor response and positive outlook. Fear and anger can be neutralized with practiced learned humor responses. We can learn to respond to adversity with humor instead of anger. Humor is a procedural skill that can be learned.

Let's look at how educators can teach humor as an alternative response pattern for kids. Walking is something we take for granted. When we trip and fall it is a pattern disruption. There are a variety of behaviors that we might exhibit, including a neutral, anger, or humor reaction. Here are some typical reactions:

☺ Ignore the action of falling.
☺ Say "darn" (or more descriptive expletive).
☺ Give a common good-natured response such as "See you next fall!" "Have a nice trip," "I'm falling for that," or some such play on words.
☺ Laugh at this unexpected challenge and one's own clumsy behavior.

What causes these differences in different people? It would seem that responses to pattern disruption are associated with the emotional pathways present in each individual's brain, including both genetic and environmental factors. The individual reaction to pattern disruption is complex. It seems plausible that the reason a certain pattern disruption is funny to one person and repulsive to another involves the hardwiring of humor responses in individual brains. The more hardwired a neural pathway is in the brain, the more difficult it will be to change the response patterns. However, it can be done.

Our ability to respond with positive energy or humergy to unexpected disruptions in patterns is an invaluable skill for the teacher's tackle box.

Humor is a procedural skill. It can be taught. Many teachers are already doing this effectively by presenting kids with options and choices. Responding with humor to the difficulties in life is a great choice. Asking a child how they could have responded with humor instead of with anger is an effective strategy.

If a child is having fun in school and if they are actively engaged in learning (as defined below in the segment on creating a nurturing environment), the chances for misbehavior decrease. The combination of skillful teacher intervention and a positive engaging environment support effective classroom management. Humor is a key element in building the positive relationships with students that will make classroom management an invisible element.

Class clowns present a unique opportunity for turning around disruptive behavior. William Purkey's 2006 book on *Teaching Class Clowns* is a great resource for capitalizing on the strengths of the clowns in your class.

I don't want to overlook the challenges of the highly disruptive, emotionally needy children who seem to be evident in increasing numbers in our schools. These children need intensive intervention and it often falls on the classroom teacher to meet the needs of these children. A sense of humor will enable the teacher to survive these challenges. The more humor resources available for teachers of special needs children, the better equipped that teacher will be to provide the resources these children need.

> "If you can dream it, you can do it. Always remember that this whole thing was started with a dream and a mouse. When people laugh at Mickey Mouse, it's because he's so human; and that is the secret of his popularity."—Walt Disney

Jest for Fun

Brainstorm the fear factors that might inhibit learning in your education setting. Each week set up a fear factor program modeled on the television program, with staff sharing strategies for surviving the fear factor. Examples would be fear of school test results or fear of noncompliance with highly qualified teacher requirements. (See figure 3-4.)

Figure 3-4.

HUMOR HELPS PEOPLE COPE

"This wallpaper is killing me. One of us will have to go."

—attributed to Oscar Wilde on his deathbed

Talk about facing the most difficult challenge of life—death—with a sense of humor. As defined in chapter 1, a sense of humor is the capacity of a human being to respond to life challenges with optimism (Morrison 2005). Our goal is to increase optimistic response patterns and positive emotionality experiences. There is often dark or sick humor in response to life tragedies. This topic is explored further in chapter 4.

"Humor can provide the healthiest and most powerful method of providing a perspective on life's difficult experiences" (Sultanoff, 1994).

Humor is often shared during extreme pattern disruptions or crisis experiences. After 9/11 there were concerns for the ability of our nation to find its sense of humor. Our perceived ability to cope was dependent on our ability to respond to a new trauma. Millions tuned in to the late night shows to see how comedians would handle the painful events. David Letterman took a week off and came back with a tribute to New York. As comedians tried to balance the grief and the need for the normalcy that humor has to offer, it was a time when humor (or lack of it) was in the forefront of our lives.

"Can we be funny? Why start now?"

—New York Mayor Rudy Giuliani, responding to a question from Saturday Night Live producer Lorne Michaels during the show's first telecast after the terrorist attacks of 9/11

"Tom Ridge announced a new color-coded alarm system. Green means everything's okay. Red means we're in extreme danger. And champagne-fuchsia means we're being attacked by Martha Stewart."

—Conan O'Brien

"This thing is so confusing. Yesterday the alert went from blue to pink; now half the country thinks we're pregnant."

—Jay Leno, on the color-coded terror alert system

Helping kids who are facing painful and life-threatening situations is the basis of a research grant that began in 2002. University of California, Los Angeles cancer researchers Margaret Stuber and Lonnie Zeltzer have launched a five-year study—dubbed Rx Laughter—to investigate the impact of humor and laughter on the immune systems of dozens of healthy children and children confronting life-threatening diseases. The first physician-researchers to look at the impact of comedy on both healthy and sick children, Stuber and Zeltzer are calling on the talents of comedy's legendary heroes to help them out.

"We're not hypothesizing that humor will be curative or that it is going to take the place of any other kind of therapy, but we [believe] that humor is going to have an additional benefit over and above simply removing or reducing stress," explains Stuber. "What I'm hoping is that we'll actually be changing the level of arousal in the autonomic nervous system, so we'll get the children to relax at that central level." (Rayl, 2002)

Humor is a strong indicator to us that we can experience life's difficulties and not only survive them but also thrive. It can allow us to detach from a crisis (large pattern disruption) for a few moments and find some hope or optimism in the situation that will relieve the stress or fears that we face (Sultanoff, 1994).

> "Today, if you invent a better mousetrap, the government comes along with a better mouse."
>
> —Ronald Reagan

Would you believe that age improves our sense of well-being and our ability to respond to challenges with humor? Aging may actually improve the positive thinking of the brain. Psychologist Daniel K. Mroczek surveyed 2,727 men and women ages 25–74 to determine how age, gender, marital status, education, health, and other factors impact well-being. He found that the aging process itself predicted a more positive mental state. "The older the person was, the more he or she reported positive emotions like cheerfulness, life satisfaction, and overall happiness within the past 30 days. And surprisingly, the younger participants reported more negative emotions, like feeling sad, nervous, hopeless or worthless" (Mroczek, 2005). Although elderly white males have the highest suicide rate of any group, Mroczek found that older men in his study, especially those who were married, reported being the happiest and having the least amount of negative emotion. Older women also reported more positive emotions than younger women. How does Mroczek account for this increase in happiness among people nearing the end of their lives?

> From our research, we have seen that older adults regulate their emotions more effectively than younger or middle-age adults. We can propose that older individuals seem to be able to know, through their years of experience, what kinds of external events increase or decrease their positive and negative emotions. Therefore, they achieve a better "emotional balance" by selecting people and situations that will minimize negative and maximize positive emotions. (Mroczek, 2005)

Once humor is established as a hardwired response pattern, a sense of humor can become a finely honed skill that enables an individual to consistently respond with optimism and humergy. When we persist at increasing the fun in our lives, we become increasingly skilled at developing our own individual humor craft.

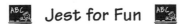 Jest for Fun

Spend more time with colleagues that you enjoy. Encourage their efforts for fun and laughter. Be sure to tell them how much you appreciate their sense of humor. We often forget to honor those who bring joy into our lives, but dwell instead on the negative feedback from negative people.

HUMOR ENHANCES THE JOY-FLOW CRAFT OF TEACHING

It is difficult to ascertain the impact that high-stakes testing is having on the culture of our schools. However, it doesn't take a rocket scientist to know that stress and burnout among educators is on the rise. Legislation that mandates increased testing of students rarely takes into account the impact it will have on the emotional well-being of our teachers and students. (See figure 3-5.)

Figure 3-5.

Table 3-1. Cultural Indicators in the Classroom

Fear-Based	Joyflow
No choice for students	Opportunities for choice
Silence emphasized	Music, conversation, laughter
Criticism	Affirmations
Teacher-centered	Student-centered
Emphasis on a reward system	Invisible discipline
Intensity	Reflection time
Little curriculum integration	Curriculum integration
Pop quizzes and grades	Performance assessment with reflective feedback
Threatening	Challenging
Low trust and low fun	High trust and lots of fun
Boredom	Engagement
Low energy	Enthusiasm and excitement
Stressful	Challenging
Fearful	Joyful

What is the current "emotional temperament" of our school systems? Questions about the intensity of the accountability movement and the resulting stress must be addressed. Mandated legislation has over-whelmed the financial and emotional resources of our educational system. Educators value accountability and they want to be sure their students are succeeding. However, increasing the amount of high-stakes testing is not always conducive to increasing student achievement. (See table 3-1.)

PROMISING RESEARCH

As mentioned in chapter 1, the Positive Emotions and Psychophysiology (PEP) Lab at the University of Michigan wants to understand and share the significance of positive emotions. This is a study of the relationship between emotion and the autonomic nervous system activity in people who flourish. Martin Seligman, former president of the American Psychological Association, uses the term "positive psychology" to identify what makes people thrive. Traditionally, psychology has focused on deficit characteristics such as anger, anxiety, and sadness. Seligman, along with Mihaly Csikszentmihalyi, who originated the concept of flow, has changed the paradigm to the study of human strengths and sources of happiness (Seligman, 2000).

Psychology previously focused on studying what was wrong with people. We often center on what students are not able to do—on what they do not know. What happens when research changes the paradigm of study to strengthening the positive attributes? A hypothesis called *broadening studies* states that "distinct, discrete positive emotions broaden the scopes of attention, cognition, and action, widening the array of percepts, thoughts, and action presently in mind. A corollary narrowing hypothesis states that negative emotions shrink these same arrays" (Seligman, 2000). "The positive emotions actually widen the opportunities for learning whereas the negative emotions narrow the options," say the folks at the PEP lab (www.lsa.umich.edu/psych/peplab/broaden.htm).

The implications of this research are critically important to educators. It gives credence to the concept of joy-flow and humergy concepts I've identified and it provides the impetus for further research on humor.

The positive emotions are more difficult to study then the negative ones since they are comparatively fewer in number and relatively undifferentiated. The optimistic emotions of joy, amusement, and humor are not as easily "read" as anger or fear. As mentioned in the research on fear, folks attend quickly to the negative emotions because they alert our attentional system to the worry about immediate survival. The positive emotions, while important for personal growth and emotional stability, do not pose this urgent need (Fredrickson, 2003).

A relatively new option for the treatment of a variety of disorders is the use of humor therapy. This treatment is based on the use of humor as a deliberate attempt to provide symptom relief and it's practiced for both physical and emotional disorders. Some therapists are experimenting with the use of humor as a treatment option for depression and mental illness. Clowns, toys, and humor resource rooms are available in some hospitals as a focus on the healing benefits of humor. While there is mounting scientific evidence that humor reduces the natural stresses of illness and distracts the patient from pain, no conclusions can yet be made as to the correlation between pain relief and humor.

Play therapy has long been used with children as a vehicle for working through emotional challenges. Play therapy is defined by the Association for Play Therapy as "the systematic use of a theoretical model to establish an interpersonal process wherein trained play therapists use the therapeutic powers of play to help clients prevent or resolve psychosocial difficulties and achieve optimal growth and development." A lay definition might be "a form of counseling that uses play to communicate with and render assistance, especially to children whose natural language is play" (en.wikipedia.org/wiki/Play_therapy).

For many folks it is difficult not to be "high on humor." There is a passion and fervor among those who believe strongly in the healing of humor. As an attendee at the Association for Applied and Therapeutic Humor conference in Chicago in 2003, I witnessed the strong negative reaction of the audience when Rod Martin presented an overview of the research that challenged some popular theories. Humor quackery is difficult to overcome. Hard research on humor is increasing, but many of the mouse droppings are scattered and inconclusive. There are a few organizations dedicated to scientific research on humor. One such organization is The International Society for Humor Studies which publishes *Humor: An International Journal of Humor Research*. Some journals that occasionally cite humor research in their publications include the *Journal of the American Medical Association*, and the *Journal of Physiology*. For a great overview of the many facets of humor, do take a look at *The Encyclopedia of 20th-Century American Humor* (Nilsen & Nilsen, 2000). And once again, for the lay practitioner who wants a quick, reliable overview of the research, I recommend the Association for Applied and Therapeutic Humor website at www.aath.org.

I'm grateful that the interest in humor research is growing. Future mouse droppings will be revealing to those who might think humor research is just a bunch of crap. Educators can be most effective when they are aware of the cognitive implications of humor research and feel confident in applying this knowledge to their practice.

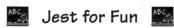 **Jest for Fun**

Share resources on humor and health. The focus of this book is humor and learning, but there is fascinating research on the healing power of humor.

SUMMARY

A staggering amount of data, emerging from biological research and from imaging technology, provides compelling evidence linking humor and learning. While it is clear that fear and stress inhibit learning, the research on humor and joy is more complex. An increasing number of studies confirm the relationship between positive emotions and learning. Here are some benefits of humor in the learning process:

- ☺ Captures and retains student attention
- ☺ Expands student comprehension
- ☺ Increases the opportunity for memory retention
- ☺ Builds relationships with students and colleagues
- ☺ Creates a nurturing environment for learning
- ☺ Supports classroom management
- ☺ Helps people cope
- ☺ Enhances the joy-flow craft of teaching

Emotions drive attention and attention drives learning. The emotion of fear has traditionally driven our school vehicles. Fear is the most frequent basis for our grading system, our discipline techniques, and the accountability movement. This fear is harbored in school cultures that reflect stress and burnout both in the teachers and students. Extreme stress is not only detrimental to a healthy lifestyle but it also decreases cognitive development: learning is inhibited in a stressful environment.

Positive emotionality (including humor) can act as a hook, line, and sinker in memory retention. Humor has the power to capture attention (hook), manipulate this information with repetition and practice in the working memory (line), and provide feedback and reflection as part of a response system (sinker). Humergy can become a component of our automated response system.

Laughter research is difficult because we all laugh at different things. We know that laughter is contagious and reflects human connections. Mirror neuron research may soon give us insights as to why we laugh with others and why humor is an important part of relationships.

Humor contributes to a healthy environment that reduces stress and increases our coping capacity. It is an indicator of our ability to survive tragedy and adapt to change. Research on humor is in the pioneering stage, but as MRI technology continues to advance we will gain further insights into the complex issues of the relationship between positive emotionality and learning.

Powerful Practice—Strategies for School Leaders

☺ Identify current staff professional development needs to find ways to keep up-to-date on the fast pace of cognitive and humor research.

☺ Find a way to share faculty resources and expertise from workshops and conferences.

☺ Encourage creative and humorous insights.

☺ Link cognitive research and humor practice into an action plan for staff development. Involve the counselors, social workers, and psychologists, inviting their insights for practical application. Check out *Layered Curriculum* by Kathie Nunley (2001) as a choice-driven and learning-focused program.

☺ Facilitate a discussion on the prevalent emotional forces at work in your system. What negative emotions are narrowing thinking and limiting opportunities for personal growth and development? What emotional impact does your accountability system have on the opportunities for positive emotionality?

☺ Encourage faculty to come to consensus on one area of humor research. Brainstorm possible ways of increasing the positive emotionality of students and faculty with the purpose of expanding thinking and increasing flow experiences.

☺ Stress relief strategies can be shared on the staff bulletin board.

☺ Pair different colleagues each month (month mates). Focus on building relationships based on fun and providing support for that person in their quest for humergy. Choose one playful or fun activity to do with that person during the month. This can be as simple as taking a walk in the gym, eating lunch together, or sharing jokes.

☺ Give each staff member the gift of a tennis ball with their name on it. A powerful self massage can be experienced when the ball is positioned between an individual and a wall or preferably the floor. This is especially relaxing for the upper back and neck muscles that can become tense during the day.

☺ If you do not have a staff exercise facility, ask for donations of good used exercise equipment to be placed in a designated exercise room (if space allows it) in your building. Encourage members to work out in the morning before school or after school with each other.

Study Group Focus

Review and discuss the research on positive emotionality at the PEP lab at the University of Michigan. For details see the website at www.lsa.umich.edu/psych/peplab/intro.htm.

Pick one of the following research topics for your group to pursue:

Positive emotionality. We all know some students who seem to have overwhelming life challenges. Spend a week observing and writing your observations on one of these children. Review your notes and decide on a plan to increase the positive emotional responses to this child. Initiate an age-appropriate discussion with this child about positive thinking and change of emotional state. Serve as a mentor and promote their attempts for change. Use the resources provided in this book and joke books, and encourage increased laughter, fun, and play. Remember to honor any tragedy that might occur with your students with the gift of time and understanding.

Memory hooks. Begin to develop humor hooks for your lessons. Look for humor everywhere. Increase your strategies for fun with purposeful attentional humor tools.

State changers. During your next staff evaluation, ask the principal to keep track of how often you changed the state of energy in your classroom.

Testing strategies. Remember the purpose of assessment is for *learning*—not grading. Authentic assessment will encourage students to do their best on their tests. Have students create their own rubrics and assessments. Try some of these options:

☺ Include an option for a lifeline or ask a friend. (This can be done midway through the test for everyone.)

☺ Include several crazy questions or responses.

☺ Have a party during state or federal testing called "Celebrate What You Know!" with balloons, nutritious snacks, or test count-down (ten days before the test—have something special each day).

Café Conversations

☺ Review the research of the PEP Lab from the University of Michigan. Discuss the implications of this research in relationship to your district goals.

☺ Share ways that colleagues use humor as a hook for learning. Explore the benefits of linking this type of learning with lesson planning.

"The early bird gets the worm, but the second mouse gets the cheese."

Chapter 4

HURTFUL HUMOR
IS NO LAUGHING MATTER

"No sense being pessimistic. It wouldn't work anyway."

Humor often emerges as a response to transitions, change events, pain, and tragedy. It's an invaluable coping response to the complex difficulties humans face. Most educators rely on their sense of humor to survive the challenges and increased demands placed on them.

There are moments in history when nations wonder if the ability to use humor has been lost to an extraordinary tragedy. During these times there appears to be a fear of laughter and our ability to use humor.

This is a time in school history when humor is vanishing and in some instances has disappeared altogether. Political mandates and increased demands on educators have been reflected in less fun, laughter, and joy in our schools. This phenomenon, rooted in our deep fears of inadequacy, is reflected in a joyless school system. The term *humorphobia* is my attempt to identify the fear of fun, laughter, and humor growing in our schools.

HUMORPHOBIA

Humorphobia is the fear of fun, laughter, and humor. Humorphobia exists as a transparent thread often woven into the fabric of our education system. Most teachers are passionate about creating a happy classroom, yet are hampered by unspoken belief systems that permeate our organizations. These fear factors include:

☹ Fear of not having time for humor because of accountability expectations.

☹ Fear of being perceived as silly, unproductive, an airhead, and unprofessional.

☹ Fear of losing "control" of the class or loss of discipline (e.g., do not smile until Christmas syndrome).

☹ Fear of inadequacy or inability to tell a joke coupled with inexperience in the use of humor (because humor is not taught or modeled in teacher preparation programs).

☹ Fear of punishment or retaliation in an environment that is hostile or unaccustomed to humor.

☹ Fear of being made fun of or being the brunt of jokes.

Humorphobia is often barely perceptible, but has a tremendous impact on humor practice. The fears that generate humorphobia create substantial barriers for creating and sustaining humergy.

Many of our fears are well founded, because education has been under attack for several decades. Political and economic forces have demanded accountability for tax dollars spent in education; the focus on assessment and teacher quality is mandated and the implementation of these laws drains our energy and resources. These demands generate increasingly stressful conditions for educators.

> "Most of the time I don't have much fun. The rest of the time I don't have any fun at all."
>
> —Woody Allen

So we have a culture that reflects our deepest fears by limiting our capacity to practice teaching and learning with joy. At the American

Association of School Administrators 2006 conference in San Diego, this loss of joyful teaching was referred to frequently by several speakers, but best captured by President David Gee when he said that one of the necessary goals of the organization was to bring joy back to education. There was an outburst of vigorous applause from the audience.

The "funny" thing is that we do not recognize how joyless our profession has become. References to the importance of having a sense of humor are liberally sprinkled throughout the literature. It is usually mentioned as a factor to look for when hiring, and briefly mentioned as one of the qualities of effective teachers in the Association for Supervision and Curriculum Development book *Qualities of Effective Teachers* (Stronge, 2004). "Effective teachers have a good sense of humor and are willing to share jokes." It is without a doubt the one quality most of us agree is needed in education. Why then is humor research and purposeful practice so limited?

HUMOR PARADOX

This is the humor paradox. We are a society that claims to place a high value on humor, but the reality is that our fears keep us from initiating and sustaining humor practice. (See figure 4-1.)

Let's take a closer look at the fear factors that inhibit humor practice.

Limited Time

Wasting learning time is a firmly established well-founded fear. It is a struggle to find the time necessary to implement instructional mandates and educators have deep concerns about their ability to accomplish all that is expected of them. Administrators, who believe in humor, use it with caution because of their very real concerns about public accountability issues. Several administrators have expressed the worry that if they are seen "goofing around," the perception will be that they aren't working. Teachers worry that if they are joking and laughing with their class, they are not preparing for tests. The message is strong and clear. *We do not have time for fun.*

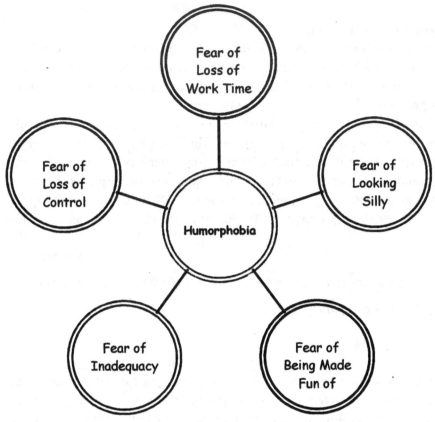

Figure 4-1. Fear factors.

"The time to laugh is when you don't have time to laugh"

—Argus Poster

Unprofessional/Childish Perceptions

There is a general societal perception that play, laughter, fun, and games are for young children. Unless teaching at the early elementary level, professional educators are generally not thought to be playful, enthusiastic, energetic, fun-loving individuals. Think of how teachers are often portrayed in the media, for example in *Ferris Bueller's Day Off*. Teachers and administrators are seen as dour, mean, and controlling. This is the pervasive image of educators, frequently perpetuated by the media.

At the beginning of the twentieth century, teachers were revered and the profession was admired, but this has changed. Education is often seen as an easy field. After all, educators only work nine months and a mere six hours a day. A variety of societal pressures have led to the struggle of educators to be seen as professionals. Politicians think it is their duty to mandate education policy when they perceive educators as incapable of making needed change. This societal pressure and stress diminishes the prospects for a joy-flow culture.

Losing Control

New teachers have often been told, "Don't smile until Christmas." The implication is that if you are seen as fun-loving, you will not have classroom control and student misbehavior will be the result. Humor is often noisy, energetic, and loud. In a culture that values quiet and order, it may appear that students are out of control. The reality is that discipline is not problematic in engaged learning classrooms where caring teachers offer students choice in the learning process. When students perceive learning as fun, student discipline is not an issue.

Humor is often seen in a negative light because of the disruption caused by a class clown. They are feared because of their ability to disrupt with their antics. An authoritarian approach to these lively youngsters is just the opposite of what is needed. Clowning is a gift. Encourage the clown to use this gift to enrich the class (Purkey, 2006). Give her opportunities to shine in the clown role. There are additional resources for clowning schools and "Clowns on Rounds" as part of a healing program in hospitals. Most retirement homes would welcome clowns visiting their residents. (Additional ideas are mentioned in chapter 6.)

Inadequacy and Inexperience

Humor is often considered an inherited trait rather then a skill that can be nurtured and developed. Humor skills as a part of teacher preparation are virtually nonexistent. In fact, since we have been programmed to believe that play and fun are immature activities, our ability to practice humor has been limited. The benefits of humor as outlined in previous chapters convince us that we need to develop humor confidence through humor practice. Chapter 5 explores a variety of ways to improve our skills and abilities. The study of humor is complex and deserves recognition as an integral part of teacher preparation programs.

Being Made Fun Of

One of the greatest fears is the fear of being laughed at. Speech classes usually begin with the recognition that many people would rather die than give a speech. No one likes to be the brunt of ridicule and the prevalence of cruel teasing increases at the middle school level. The dark humor of sarcasm, mockery, and ridicule are controlling tactics used by bullies to manipulate their victims.

Many educators have been ridiculed for attempts to have fun and use humor. Teachers often feel they can only use humor behind the closed door of their classroom, because they feel safe there. This closed door safety is diminishing as collaborative teaching has been promoted as an effective way to maximize achievement, but collaboration can be an effective tool for teachers to support each other in humor practice. Study groups and café conversations are formats included in this book for this purpose. "I have fun with my kids after I close the door and I am sure that no one can hear the laughter," an elementary teacher at a humor workshop said.

The challenges of addressing humorphobia cannot be overestimated. When these fears are deep-seated in an individual and firmly rooted within an organization, a few fun activities will not begin to address the complexity of the issues. The benefits of humor (chapter 1) must be studied in our teacher preparation programs and supported in our schools' mentoring programs. Novice teachers desperately need the benefits that humor can provide for them in their first years of teaching. Awareness of humorphobia and identification of these fears are crucial in the ability to create a culture that supports humergy.

"Everything is funny as long as it is happening to someone else."

—Will Rogers

Jest for Fun

Cherish the class clowns. You may have a future Robin Williams, Richard Pryor, or Lucille Ball in your class. Picture your clown as a star.

ADDRESSING HUMORPHOBIA

Observe and record the evidence of humorphobia in your workplace. Over time, humorphobia can become an integral part of the negativity of individuals and impact the entire system. Awareness of fears, commitment to change, and focused staff development are preliminary steps in building the confidence needed to revive the energy of humor. The level of trust in an organization can be measured by the amount of humergy that exists there. As mentioned in previous chapters, fun is an indicator of trust. An environment of trust is critical for optimal learning to occur. Listening for the language of humorphobia is a helpful step in becoming more aware of how our fears are verbalized.

- ☹ We need to be professional here. What will the public think if we are having fun and laughing?
- ☹ You must be from the elementary grades; fun just doesn't have a place at the *higher* levels.
- ☹ We cannot measure humor. It's "soft data" and not meaningful in education. We only operate from solid research.
- ☹ We don't have time for fun and games. Let's just get this meeting over with.
- ☹ I don't do "touchy feely."
- ☹ I've tried humor before and it didn't work!
- ☹ Don't smile until Christmas.

Humorphobia gives some powerful insights into the resistance encountered by enthusiastic educators trying to nurture a positive climate. If you've heard the above statements, if you've ever been called a "Pollyanna" or a "Mary Poppins" or labeled as "elementary," you have encountered humorphobia.

"A closed mouth gathers no foot."

STRATEGIES TO COMBAT HUMORPHOBIA

A commitment to the change process is required to address the deep-rooted issues of humorphobia. Skillful leaders will:

- ☺ Build a passionate belief that humergy facilitates teaching and learning
- ☺ Provide the groundwork to analyze and learn from fear factors
- ☺ Offer ongoing staff development opportunities for systemic change

Various ideas to combat humorphobia are:

- ☺ Staff institute day. Watch the *FISH* video—form *four focus groups* based on the tenants—play, choose your attitude, be there, and make their day. Have each group focus on fun ways their group can improve school climate throughout the school year.
- ☺ Teacher study groups that meet on a regular basis to read and plan activities to address culture issues. Suggested resources are *Fun Works* by Leslie Yerkes (2001), *Making Humor Work* by Terry L. Paulson (1989), and the book you're holding right now.
- ☺ Study groups or café conversations, which are included at the end of each chapter.

 Jest for Fun

Give the gift of humor. For birthdays, holidays, and special occasions give a joke book, perform a skit, or provide another humorous present. Comic strip newspaper makes great gift wrap.

"Things are going to get a lot worse before they get worse."

—Lily Tomlin

HUMORDOOMERS

Humorphobia breeds humordoomers. Humorphobia impacts both the educator and education systems by undermining teacher confidence, stifling creativity, and sabotaging humor practice. Working long and hard seems to be the societal norm for proving commitment and effectiveness. Time is a precious commodity and the increased demands require educators to make every minute count.

A humordoomer is a person who consistently uses negative humor to control and manipulate others. Humorphobia breeds humordoomers, skilled crafters who use subtle techniques to suppress humor in the workplace. Humordoomers are usually unhappy individuals stressed by the dual demands of accountability and limited time constraints; they're pessimistic leeches who can suck the humergy right out of you. Grown in a petri dish of fear and anger, these folks are threatened by joyful energy and enthusiasm. They often use humor to manipulate others and to maintain a level of control of their world. Their negative humor reflects their unhappy immersion in the confining straits of a workaholic world. Often their techniques are so woven into the fabric of a culture that not only are they unaware of their own webbing effect, their unsuspecting prey are oblivious as well.

In an article in *School Administrator*, Michael R. Weber (2003) addresses the "draining effect" that negative people have on everybody and everything. As Weber says, they consume the energy of the entire staff, negating new ideas and programs. He thinks that any effort to convert these malcontents is extremely difficult because you cannot force people to change. *Note: recognize that we can all exhibit humordoomer behavior at times, as a result of anger or fear and stress.*

An angry educator confronted me about the icebreaker activity used at a regional curriculum meeting. "Please do not use your *cutesy kindergarten stuff* at our meetings. We just do not have time." I was genuinely puzzled. This activity was designed as a pair/share networking task to introduce members to each other. The majority of the group visibly enjoyed the purposefully planned games and activities; however, even after carefully defining the goals of the activities, this encounter was the beginning of my understanding of the impact of humordoomers.

Although we know how important it is to laugh and possess a sense of humor, humorphobia creeps into the culture. Educators are stressed and concerned about their abilities to meet the accountability mandates while budgets continue to be cut. Educators are expected to raise test scores. When resources are scarce, anxiety increases and the resulting stress boils over into the culture, increasing the rising plague of burned-out educators. Cognitive research clearly demonstrates the detrimental impact excess stress has on teaching and learning.

A focus on quality teaching has generated various techniques to try to "improve" teacher effectiveness. Entire books are written with step-by-step instructions on evaluation techniques meant to *change* teacher behavior.

"The beatings will continue until morale improves!"

Punitive measures originally designed to force improvements increase the toxins in the culture. Teachers feel not only unappreciated, but also punished by negative evaluations and a disapproving public. Local newspaper articles tout the short teacher day and high teacher pay. School boards under tremendous budget restraints are often forced to make cuts that result in larger class size and tension frequently emerges between unions and administration.

Perceived punitive measures intensify feelings of fear and anger, while anger that is unresolved intensifies the bitterness, rage, and even violence. Deep-seated anger manifests itself in many ways. Negative humor may be used to express frustration, hostility, fears, and anger. If one feels inferior, laughing at others becomes a way to feel superior and can become a weapon in the hands of stressed unhappy individuals. Control and power are the goals of those who use humor to evoke feelings of fear and distress in others. Humor that is sarcastic, cynical, or mocking results in the recipient feeling helpless and vulnerable.

There are two indicators of unresolved anger that can be identified and observed in both adult and student behavior. Educators, familiar with these categories, can view behavior through the humor lens:

☹ Bullying
☹ Victimization

As we struggle to teach students about the roles of bully and victim, it behooves us to become aware of similar practices exhibited by adults. Numerous insights emerge when looking at these characteristics through the lens of humor.

CHARACTERISTICS OF HUMORDOOMERS

The Bully

A bullying type of humor can be used to control what happens in relationships. When making fun of others, the bully is usually expressing internal fears because they are unable or unwilling to recognize their own emotional needs. Humor becomes a weapon of the bully, when used with the intentional purpose of wounding another.

Bully behavior is frequently portrayed in the media as an acceptable method to express frustration, hostility, fears, and anger. The use of mockery and sarcasm allows the venting of anger. Jokes with the express purpose of making fun of others abound on television, in movies, and on the Internet. Our fears of difference in culture have often been expressed in jokes about Italians, Jews, Mexicans, gays, and religious entities. While often clever, these jokes perpetuate the bully mindset that it's okay to make fun of individuals or groups. There is previous research to suggest that this type of humor can lead to violent behavior.

"The devaluation of racial ethnic or religious groups, sometimes disguised as humor, is a major contributor to violence and aggression against these groups. It was found that emotional empathy was negatively correlated only with the humorousness of negative ethnic stereotype jokes" (Forsyth, Altermatt, & Forsyth, 1997).

The Victim

The recipient of bullying feels powerless. The fear of being made fun of can strip away confidence and the ability to make positive changes, and legislative mandates and funding inequities have resulted in loss of power and hope for many educators. Victims emerge who blame others for difficulties, acquire a learned response of helplessness, feel they have no control over their lives, and operate out of deep fear and anxiety. They do not appear to enjoy life and constantly remind others of their own difficulties.

One of my vivid memories is a dreary January day when I thought it would be fun to brighten our week and suggested having a Hawaiian luncheon. "Sure must be nice not to have anything to do," was the reaction of a coworker to the suggestion. It was obvious she had so much work that she had no time for anything fun, and she didn't approve of others wasting their time on frivolous matters. This use of sarcasm can be a powerful negative force within a system.

Jest for Fun

The inside doors of the staff restroom stalls are an ideal place for jokes, reminders, and stories. One community college called this restroom news marketing tool "The Flush."

UNCOVERING THE TRANSPARENT LANGUAGE OF HUMORDOOMERS

The bully:

- ☹ Do you think you're in this class to have fun?
- ☹ Wipe that smile off your face!
- ☹ Stop fooling around and get to work.
- ☹ You could do it if you didn't play around so much.
- ☹ Name calling: You're so "derogatory statement" (stupid, ugly, white, fat, etc.).
- ☹ Mockery, exaggeration of a behavior such as walking or speech.
- ☹ Ridicule of clothing (for example, too short slacks "You expecting a flood?" or a sports coat "You going to a funeral?")

The victim:

- ☹ Great. I have the class clown.
- ☹ Don't smile until Christmas.
- ☹ Kids today have no respect.
- ☹ I teach it, it's up to the kids to learn it.
- ☹ Do you have to be so perky?
- ☹ Quit being a Pollyanna and get real. You can't make this place any better.
- ☹ Don't do so much, you'll make the rest of us look like couch potatoes.
- ☹ Oh sure, now they want us to use humor with our students. Like we don't already have enough to do.

If challenged, the humordoomer usually responds with, "Can't you take a joke?" or "I was just playing with you." Often a clever ruse is the blame technique, in which the humordoomer accuses the challenger of having no sense of humor by saying she can't take a joke. This is intended to excuse offensive behavior, while putting the recipient on the defensive.

"If you find yourself in a hole, stop digging." —Will Rogers

COPING WITH HUMORDOOMERS

While difficult to deal with, there are some strategies that you can use to stimulate humordoomer reform. Attempt to identify the cause of the negative behavior exhibited by humordoomers and follow this with suggestions for change. This requires a loving attitude and skillful communication. (Note: these negative patterns of behavior are usually hardwired after years of repetition.) The following are strategies to combat *stressed humordoomers* (who are fearful and overwhelmed):

☺ Kill them with kindness and understanding. Often people need someone to listen to them and empathize.

☺ Identify the strengths in this person and tell them how much you appreciate this quality in them. It really helps if you have several staff members doing this.

☺ Ask them what they are going to do to make things better. Encourage any attempts at improvement.

The following are strategies for *pessimistic humordoomers* (who are habitually negative):

☺ Smile and say "If you tell me something awful, I need you to tell me three positive things. I just can't handle negativity today!"

☺ Do the broken record routine: "So what's the *good* news?" Just keep repeating this with a laugh. If they come up with something positive, cheer and do cartwheels!

And the way to combat *angry humordoomers* (resentful and frustrated with lack of control in their life and unable to express their feelings in positive ways) is to recognize that these folks may actually need more help then you are able to give. If you have the opportunity, suggest that they seek counseling and/or therapy.

Although I usually think of something clever *after* my encounters with negative people, there are some one-liners that you can experiment with.

☺ I resemble that statement.
☺ Start today with a smile and get it over with.
☺ There's no time like the pleasant.
☺ If you don't learn to laugh at trouble, you won't have anything to laugh at when you are old.—Ed Howe
☺ In life, pain is inevitable, but suffering is optional.—Hedy Schliefer
☺ Life is wonderful, without it you're dead.—Red Skelton
☺ When does the fun start?
☺ Don't take life too seriously; you'll never get out alive.

If you find one that you like, use the broken record routine. Use the line *every* time negative humor is encountered.

DESTRUCTIVE GAMES EDUCATORS PLAY

Clue. This game is played very well by folks who become passive aggressive. They don't give many clues as to why they are angry, they just say and do things to let you know they aren't happy with you. You haven't a *clue*!

Outburst. The purpose of this game is to control what others say and do. The object of this game is to instill in others a fear of their temper. They threaten folks with their well-known quickness for an angry tirade or outburst.

Blame game. This is the game where the person is unable to take responsibility for any of their own behavior, but blames the parents, the students, administrators, their own friends and family, the government, the media, etc. for their deficiencies.

Troubles. The rules of this game are simple. Think about every possible thing that can go wrong, exaggerate the possibilities, and live in fear and worry that big troubles will happen right here in "River City."

Scrabble. This game is also played by victims. Whatever suggestions are offered as possible solutions to their litany of difficulties, they say "Yes, but I cannot do that because . . . " or "Yes, but I know someone who tried that and it made it worse . . . " They scrabble their word options to always spell the word *"no."*

Monopoly. This game is played by victims who think they have it worse then anyone else. They have a monopoly on difficulties. If you ever mention that you're tired and have a lot of papers to grade in the evening, their response is: "You're lucky you don't have my classes, I have 238 papers to grade tonight, and then I have wrestling practice and a meeting with a parent. When I go home I need to make a casserole for the church supper. My mother has to have bunion surgery, my car is out of gas, and we have to go to Florida for winter break again this year." Whatever your own difficulties, this victim lets you know that they have it much worse.

Taboo. This is played by folks who avoid facing problems and consider it taboo to discuss their anxieties with you. Most topics are taboo including their bullying behavior and their offensive humor techniques of mockery, sarcasm, or ridicule.

There are actually some individuals who are adept at playing several of these games at the same time.

🔲 Jest for Fun 🔲

Share the list of destructive games at a staff meeting. Ask staff which game they would most like to plan or play. Group staff with their game choice and have them actually come up with rules, game pieces, and the winning strategies. Share the ideas with other staff. Hopefully the laughter generated can initiate a serious look at existing negative tendencies.

"It's what you learn after you know it all that counts."

—John Wooden

Figure 4-2. Even if the intents is not to harm, if the impact is harmful it is inappropriate humor.

INTENT VS. IMPACT

When the impact of humor is hurtful, the humor is inappropriate even if the intent was not to harm. So, the impact of the humor on the recipient is more important then the intent of the relater. (See figure 4-2.)

The impact of humor on a group is less damaging than humor targeted at a person as an individual. There is a difference between Jay Leno offending those of your gender on national television and having a significant person in your life tell you the same thing. Read these quips, first as heard from Jay on national television, and then again as if your spouse was the speaker.

☺ I just got a dog for my wife. Best trade I ever made.
☺ I still miss my ex-husband, but my aim will improve.
☺ If we can put a *man* on the *moon* why not *all* of them?

The change in focus is significant. There are moron, blond, Polack, and fat people jokes that are usually not taken seriously; however, an awareness of the impact on the targeted population is an essential humor skill.

"When used as a weapon, humor can wound, corrupt, and humiliate. Yet, when used as a tool, humor can establish rapport, educate audiences, and empower people."

—Jessica McCann

JUST ON THE EDGE: DARK HUMOR

Sarcasm, mockery, and irony can have a purpose, when skillfully used, to cope with stress, challenge beliefs, and criticize the behavior of others without offending. This type of edgy humor does capture our attention and can cause us to reflect and rethink our beliefs. Don and Alleen Nilsen have written *The Encyclopedia of 20th-Century American Humor* (2000), a great resource for humor research. They state that several comedians and humorists have achieved popularity by using ethnic humor and stereotyping—even vulgarity—to win an audience. African-American comedians like Richard Pryor, Eddie Murphy, Whoopi Goldberg, and Chris Rock use comedy to tease listeners about their prejudices. Jay Leno and Dave Letterman use the daily news and politics as the basis for their opening monologues with jokes laced with satire and irony.

Don Nilsen identifies political correctness as avoiding any language or action that could offend one's political sensibilities. He says that

> political correctness stunts the many positive opportunities that humor has to offer. It is censorship that bans all stereotyping, ethnic jokes, religious humor and vulgarity. Censorship from the *conservative right* says we must not use profanity or joke about body parts, bodily functions, or religion. Censorship from the *liberal left* spells out a whole different set of taboos, making gender issues and ethnicity entirely off limits.

Ethnic humor and stereotyping can vary from playful teasing to a more hostile humor. The difference between humor intended to seriously wound and purposeful humor used as a skillful tool to facilitate change can be subtle. When trying to decide if humor is appropriate, use the following guideline: *even if the intent is not to hurt, if the impact is hurtful, it is not appropriate.*

"It infuriates me to be wrong when I know I am right."

KIDDING AND TEASING

One day my five-year-old grandsons were eating breakfast in the kitchen. I sang a silly song. At the end, I said: "Ben, you have purple teeth and Tyler, you have green ears!" One of them responded that it was not nice to tease. Obviously their kindergarten teachers were doing a great job of making sure that there was no harmful teasing in their classrooms. We then had a discussion about bad teasing being the kind that hurts a person's feelings and how it's different than fun kidding when someone is trying to make you laugh or have a good time with you. It occurred to me that this was a discussion about impact versus intent on a rudimentary level.

Teasing is often used by teachers to help a child laugh at their own behavior (a fundamental skill). It is a highly developed ability in gifted teachers. Remember the *impact vs. intent* rule. If the child is really able to enjoy the humor then the teasing is okay. It takes careful observation techniques to determine if a child is okay with gentle kidding and teasing.

> "After eating an entire bull, a mountain lion felt so good he started roaring. He kept it up until a hunter came along and shot him. The moral: When you're full of bull, keep your mouth shut."
>
> —Will Rogers

Jest for Fun

Looking for a fundraiser? Have a roast for the famous graduates of your school system. Make sure they understand they will be the recipients of this type of humor.

GROUP SURVIVAL HUMOR

Group survival humor emerges from coping with someone who is hostile toward the group or from unwelcome change. Hostile jokes target those in power who have caused difficulty for the group. This group survival humor seems to relieve stress and ease group sense of a loss of control. This humor often strengthens group bonds and further alienates the authority figure. Numerous jokes found on the Internet target people in power.

Doctor Jokes

> "All of them surgeons, they're highway robbers. Why do you think they wear masks when they work on you?"
>
> —Archie Bunker

"I told my doctor I had suicidal tendencies. He said that from now on I have to pay in advance."

—Rodney Dangerfield

Administrator Jokes

"She brings a lot of joy whenever she leaves the room."

"If you gave him a penny for his thoughts, you'd get change."

"She doesn't have ulcers but she is a carrier."

"He sets low personal standards and constantly fails to achieve them."

Politician Jokes

"If ignorance is bliss, then Congress must be paradise."

"It's 98 percent of politicians that give the rest a bad name."

"The trouble with political jokes is how often they get elected."

"Lady Astor once told Winston Churchill, 'If you were my husband, I would put poison in your coffee!' Churchill is said to have immediately responded, 'If you were my wife, I would drink it.'"

LAUGHTER AND TEARS

"Comedy is tragedy plus time." —Carol Burnett

There is a delicate balance between laughter and tears. Can humor be effective when coping with death, sickness, depression, anxiety, and other life challenges? Humor usually emerges during a healthy healing process. Forced laughter or contrived humor is often inappropriate, so great caution must be exercised in using humor during tragic situations. Having said this, humor is a great healer during times of disaster and grief.

At Maple Elementary School in Loves Park, Illinois, a 6th grade teacher, Andrea Sweet, was diagnosed with cancer and underwent chemotherapy. Her situation was obvious due to her loss of hair and wearing of hats. She encouraged her students to join in her coping strategies by laughing with her. Her room is often permeated with this laughter. When Halloween came she read the story "Witches," listing ways that people can identify witches. One of the items was loss of hair. When I first met Andrea, she had just read the book and was laughing that the students were now sure that she was a witch. The principal of the building, Becky Girard, stated that for the school picture, all of the teachers wore hats as a tribute to this teacher who has inspired everyone in the building with her infectious laughter and sense of humor.

Another teacher in the building was introduced to a new student, a boy with extreme ADHD. After the interview she burst into laughter and explained, "I can either laugh or cry. I choose to find the joy and laughter in this child along with the gifts that he will bring to our class." This building exemplifies the culture of humergy that is so needed in our school systems. Looking for the ways to laugh through the difficult experiences that we all encounter and sharing those coping mechanisms with others will build the communities of trust and joy that maximize learning.

> "Life does not cease to be funny when someone dies, anymore then it ceases to be serious when someone laughs."
>
> —George Bernard Shaw

SUMMARY

An awareness of humorphobia is necessary to begin to integrate humergy into school climate. The fear factors that impact humorphobia are concerns with time, professionalism, lack of classroom control, inexperience, and being made fun of. These fears contribute to the challenges of school leaders trying to integrate humor into a school culture.

Resistance to change is often exhibited as humorphobia. Humor-doomers are negative folks who sabotage efforts to infuse fun and laughter into the culture. Positive efforts by visionary leaders can assist most in the change process, so staff development focused on creating play, laughter, and fun to optimize learning is an effective tool. However, often the bully and victim negativity needs to be confronted by identifying specific behaviors and concerns accompanied by suggestions for improvement. Change for the most dysfunctional individuals might only be achieved through counseling.

Humor is an integral component of our whole emotional and intellectual lives, both at the individual and organizational level. Humorphobia and humordoomers create a *no fun* restrictive learning environment. These barriers need to be addressed in order to create the positive emotionality and relational trust necessary for optimal learning.

Powerful Practice—Strategies for School Leaders

☺ Recognize that effective leadership can jumpstart humordoomer recovery. The fear of using humor stems from the fact that it is not a *controlled substance.* To practice humor, one has to be willing to let go and enjoy some degree of chaos. Humor requires risk taking. It involves not just acceptance, but actually searching for the excitement that change generates. It seeks the unexpected and reveres uncertainty. As education has become more and more demanding, it has not only inhibited humergy, but also has created a hostile environment for humor practice.

☺ Generate staff discussion on how the organization can cultivate the risk taking required to support humor practice. Some effective strategies might include theme weeks, which can generate creativity among all of the staff, such as Hawaiian Week or Childhood Games Week (hula hoops, jacks, tiddlywinks, checkers, or tic-tac-toe contests), and a Fourth of July in January party.

Study Group Focus

☺ Humorphobia can be challenging for both teachers and students. Review strategies for addressing humor fears. Share observations of what might work in your culture to address student fears.

☺ Keep a journal for one week of the type of humor observed on television. Discuss any insights relative to the information found in this chapter.

☺ Share any strong reactions you had to the information in this chapter. Relate past experiences that illustrate something that triggered this reaction.

Café Conversations

☺ One of the greatest fears we have is a dread of being laughed at. Bullies often manipulate others through this fear by threatening others with sarcasm and ridicule, and most of us avoid these people. A discussion question might be: what observations have been made about humor used as a vehicle for bullies?

☺ Attempts at humor during a crisis situation can be experienced by those immersed in that crisis as insensitive and even hurtful. We are afraid to use humor in crisis in the belief that it will hurt rather than help others. This was well documented during 9/11, when talk show hosts, normally skilled humorists, were painfully uncomfortable in using humor immediately after this tragedy. How have you used humor in a crisis?

☺ Discuss the impact of negative humor. What impact does the humordoomer have on a culture of a school? What are the options for changing the behavior of a humordoomer?

"I am not pessimistic, I am optimistically challenged."

Chapter 5

THE HUMOR WORKOUT

Pumping Up with Practice

"Whenever I feel blue, I just start breathing again."

Jest do it. Determination and resolution are all you need to start your humor workout. The actual decision to pump up your humor practice can be similar in scope to the decision of including more physical fitness in your life. This is a powerful choice that can improve your sense of humor and increase your capacity for reaching the joy-flow stage. Do not let anything deter you from your goal to have more fun. Let the workout begin!

I. GATHER BASELINE HUMOR DATA

The first step for your humor workout is an awareness of your current humor practice, in other words finding out about your own sense of humor. There are several resources available for you as you begin your analysis. Some have already been mentioned in previous chapters. Review one or several of these tools to help determine your humor strengths, humor techniques, and humergy needs. The instruments will give you some insights into your preferred humor style and your humor belief system. They are intended to help you assess the condition of your current humor health.

Assessment Tools

- ☺ Appendix 2: Comedian List
- ☺ Appendix 5: Humor Styles Inventory
- ☺ Appendix 6: Several Categories of Humor
- ☺ Appendix 7: Humor Belief Inventory
- ☺ Appendix 8: Humor Terminology List
- ☺ Table 1-1: Humergy Characteristics (in chapter 1)

Here are a few additional resources that you might want to explore:

- ☺ The University of Michigan Positive Organizational Scholarship has a Teaching Tool Series "The Reflected Best Self Exercise" (www.bus.umich.edu/Positive/WhatisPOS) that provides feedback to people about who they are when they're at their best. The focus is to identify unique strengths and talents.
- ☺ The Humor Styles Questionnaire assesses four dimensions relating to individual differences in uses of humor. (Rod A. Martin, Department of Psychology, University of Western Ontario, rmartin@uwo.ca.)

Observe Humor Practice

Efforts to become aware of your own humor practices will give you invaluable data. Think about when and how you play, laugh, and have fun. It may feel awkward at first, but keeping a humor journal is the best way to record what tickles your funny bone. For a week, just jot down what you found humorous. After a month of making a conscious effort to increase your fun, reread your entries and try the journal recording again. Are you laughing more now? What makes you laugh the most often?

Humor practice often involves overcoming your own fears of feeling silly or inept. As mentioned in previous chapters, humor requires a certain amount of risk taking. A lot of folks practice what I call *safe humor.* They feel safe laughing only in the following situations:

☺ With children
☺ With animals
☺ With strangers
☺ With drugs or alcohol
☺ With sarcasm or hurtful humor

A review of each of these categories can increase your awareness of your own comfort level with humor practice. Most educators have chosen the field of education because being with students brings joy to their lives. Children allow us to experience our own inner child, delighting adults with their language innocence and honest appraisal of a situation. Teachers sharing the innocent word twists of one of the students will cause the staff to be doubled over in hysterical laughter. Children invite us to experience humor in numerous ways.

The playful antics of pets have been shown to increase the laughter in a household. Pets provide unconditional acceptance and tremendous comfort to their owners. The ability to laugh and find common ground with others through the activity of animals creates bonds that are strengthened through stories and conversation. Several recent articles in the popular press have indicated that animals add to the quality and length of life.

Have you ever been on an airplane with a complete stranger and laughed about experiences that you might never be able to relate with family or friends? There is a degree of safety and comfort in talking with people we know we will never see again. Strangers are great secret keepers. We can tell them anything and may share the bizarre behaviors of our friends and family. This is all done within the safe comfort of the airplane seat or wherever we have those conversations with strangers.

Alcohol or substance abuse is readily accepted by society as an excuse for silly or uninhibited behavior. As detailed in chapter 2, play is generally not an acceptable outlet for teenagers and adults. We frequently seek approval or permission from our peers in order to have fun. Societal language that revolves around drugs and alcohol reflects the perceived need for a "substance" in order to let go of inhibitions enough to indulge in silly behavior. We often hear the phrase, "I couldn't help it, I was wasted!" or "I can't wait to get bombed!" There is a subtle language revolving around alcohol use that includes a purposeful loss of responsibility for one's actions as a result of excessive imbibing. Alcohol is often seen as a necessary ingredient in order to have fun. The underlying societal pressure to drink in order to "loosen up and have fun" leads to my questions about this cultural phenomenon:

Why do our youth and many adults think that a "good time" is associated with getting drunk or binge drinking? Does the extinction of play among our youth lead to increased risk of substance usage?

I have not found anything in the literature about the correlation between alcohol consumption and the extinction of play (as defined in chapter 2). Binge drinking and partying are viewed by many young adults as the ultimate kind of fun. Is it probable that we have essentially extinguished the opportunity during the preteen years for healthy fun with free-time for play. The relationship between humorphobia and substance abuse would be an intriguing topic for further research. Is it possible that risk-taking patterns of youth, including substance abuse, are a direct result of the early extinguishing of play and fun?

Making fun of others can become a habit at an early age and this form of safe humor is readily accepted in our culture. Ridiculing others is pervasive in the media. Many schools have implemented programs to teach about bullying behavior, because one of the most frequent and accepted forms of humor is cruel teasing and harassment. Laughing at other people can become habitual and indicates unhealthy patterns of behavior. As mentioned in chapter 4, this form of humor is really not funny and is often malicious and controlling. It is usually practiced by humor-doomers, the insecure individuals mentioned previously.

If you practice safe humor as just described, try expanding your humor experiences. Although there are benefits to several aspects of safe humor, you can benefit from a humor workout that is outside of your comfort zone.

Review Nature and Nurture Elements

Humor involves making the most of what has shaped our humor being. The following personal elements contribute to the nature and nurture of our sense of humor:

☺ Physical characteristics
☺ Gender

☺ Culture
☺ Life experiences: childhood, parenthood, health and aging, work, and career

Let's examine each of the nature and nurture elements:

Physical Characteristics Love your body. Your shape or size lends itself to the ability to create humor highlighting on our physical abilities. Not too many of us have a Marilyn Monroe or Elvis type of body. Our physique gives us a unique opportunity for self-deprecating humor. Several comedians have used this as a starting point for their monologues, including Jay Leno who takes advantage of his long chin and Phyllis Diller who demeans her body type, shape, and hair color.

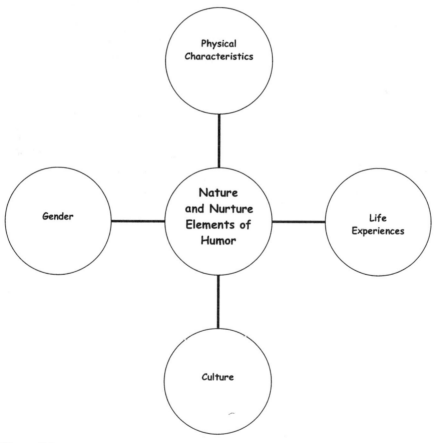

Figure 5-1.

The humor categories of slapstick, pantomime, and impersonation can be physically demanding and require an athletic build. Clown personas are often developed based on body build and type. My favorite quote illustrating self-deprecating humor:

> "I am not offended by all of the dumb blond jokes, because I know I'm not dumb. I also know I'm not blond"
>
> —Dolly Parton

People with disabilities have the unique chance to use their "handicap" as an advantage. Kathy Buckley is a popular comedian who uses her hearing impairment as a part of her comedy routines. When I heard her at the Humor Project Conference she integrated her school experiences as a part of her material. In second grade she was put in a school for retarded children because of her speech and hearing loss. It took nearly a year to diagnose the auditory impairment. After telling this story, her quip is, "And they called *me* slow?"

Gender   Men and women respond differently to humor. *Duh*. Males score higher than females on aggressive and self-defeating humor when using a Humor Styles Questionnaire (Martin, 1996). Gender differences are apparent in some of the emerging research on humor perceptions and usage (Martin, 2007). It has been perceived as more difficult for women to succeed as comedians and humorists because of traditional gender roles and expectations.

Most of us frequently receive the male/female bashing jokes that travel the e-waves and reveal the depth of feelings about gender differences and relationship issues.

☺ He said, "What have you been doing with all the grocery money I gave you?" She said, "Turn sideways and look in the mirror."
☺ Get a new car for your spouse. It'll be a great trade.
☺ Sometimes I wake up grumpy, other times I let her sleep.
☺ I still miss my ex-husband, but my aim will improve
☺ A man's got to do what a man's got to do. A woman must do what he can't.
☺ Don't be sexist. Broads hate that.

Culture Humor can reflect cultural and ethnic differences. Laughter transcends cultural boundaries when the humor is universal in nature and part of all human experiences. Many jokes have been targeted toward ethnic groups (Polish jokes) or religious groups ("Have you heard the one about the minister, the rabbi, and the priest?"). There are times when stereotypes are used as an advantage to poke fun at traditional prejudices, because it's more acceptable for an Asian comedian to poke fun at Asian culture than for someone of another ethnic background to do so. Another example is Ole and Lena stories, which are frequently told by Norwegians as well as recounted on the *Prairie Home Companion* live radio broadcast, which originates in Minnesota, home of many of Norwegian descent. This is an example of how a culture pokes fun at itself.

☺ Ole and Lena went to the Olympics. While he was sitting on a bench, a lady turned to Ole and said, "Are you a pole vaulter?" Ole said, "No, I'm Norvegian . . . and my name isn't Valter."

☺ Ole bought Lena a piano for her birthday. A few weeks later, Lars inquired how she was doing with it. "Oh," said Ole, "I persuaded her to svitch to a clarinet." "How come?" asked Lars. "Vell," Ole answered, "because vith a clarinet she can't sing."

Temperament Chapter 2 presents an overview of some of the inherited characteristics that affect humor, including intensity, adaptability, and approachability. Each trait creates a different quality of humor in individuals. These temperamental traits are reflected in common terminology used to describe someone as having a "dry" sense of humor or being a prankster or practical joker. Our temperament is the underlying basis for our humor style, but it also might create a gulf of separation between people who have completely different responses to a joke or story.

Have you ever been laughing hysterically at something and then noticed that no one else is even smiling? Differences in temperament probably contribute to our widely diverse humor responses and our clear preference for certain categories of humor (appendix 6). It behooves us to understand our temperament in order to complete the database analysis of our humor practice.

Life Experiences   Our life experiences continue to expand our humor workout. Your database needs to include your core life experiences (such as parenting, friends, and hobbies), which have enriched your sense of humor. Your humor style has its foundation in your lifelong experiences.

Childhood. My father, Bill Wiltz, enjoyed laughing with others. Whether he encountered friends or strangers, he was laughing within a few minutes and so were the other people. He didn't really tell jokes, but just visibly enjoyed life, often repeating many of the same lines over and over again, always followed by his own hearty laughter. Many of those lines involved gentle inclusion of my mother, Ruth, who admirably tolerated his quips. She was the love of his life and he was especially delighted when he made her laugh. The laughter experiences from my childhood were a powerful force in my own humor development. Many of the Wiltz clan shared this infectious laugh.

If you experienced a lot of fun, play, and laughter during childhood, your humor style will be different than if you grew up with humorphobia or an absence of fun and laughter.

The cognitive emotional responses of our childhood become part of our humor being. If our lifelong experiences include a tendency to blame others, or to feel victimized, helpless, and angry, it will be a challenge to move toward humergy. Self-awareness and acceptance of all of our feelings require intensive work, perhaps even therapy. If we understand our own painful feelings of fear and anger, we are much more likely to have a healthy humor workout. This self-analysis requires forgiveness of those who have hurt us as well as a forgiveness of ourselves. Unhealthy humordoomer behaviors are described in chapter 4. Dark, negative humor emerges from anger when forgiveness has not occurred. Incredible strength is needed to understand our own emotional reactions because it requires positive emotionality and a high level of self-confidence to laugh at our own feelings of fear or inadequacy. Overcoming our own fears might be the most difficult part of the humor workout experience. (Some of you might think sit-ups are easier!)

Parenthood. During one of my workshop sessions, a teacher (who was not a parent) noticed that parent jokes were funnier if you *were* a parent. This was the story she noticed that parents found hilarious and non-parents found somewhat funny. (Many did not have an experience to make this humor connection.)

Ham Sandwich

As ham sandwiches go, it was perfection; a thick slab of ham, a fresh bun, crisp lettuce and plenty of expensive, light brown, gourmet mustard. The corners of my jaw aching in anticipation, I carried it to the picnic table in our backyard, picked it up with both hands but was stopped by my wife suddenly at my side. "Hold Johnny (our six-week-old son) while I get my sandwich," she said.

I had him balanced between my left elbow and shoulder and was reaching again for the ham sandwich when I noticed a streak of mustard on my fingers.

I love mustard.

I had no napkin.

I licked it off.

It was not mustard.

No man ever put a baby down faster.

It was the first and only time I have sprinted with my tongue protruding. With a washcloth in each hand I did the sort of routine shoeshine boys do, only I did it on my tongue. Later my wife said, "Now you know why they call that mustard 'Poupon.'"

Here are a few other examples of parent humor:

We childproofed our homes, but they are still getting in.

If you have a lot of tension and you get a headache, do what it says on the aspirin bottle: "take two aspirin" and "keep away from children!"

This is another great story about parenting from colleague Shirley Hardy:

Nothing can be more embarrassing than getting locked outside in your birthday suit. Years ago when my daughter was just a toddler she helped me to do so. We had just come home for the evening after a tedious day. I started the shower to begin our usual evening ritual of shower then bed. I undressed myself, then her, and suddenly remembered I forgot her new box of Pampers in the car. Being that I had a private backyard, I thought I could dash to the car get the Pampers and commence the shower.

On the way back into the house I heard *slam*! My ten-month-old daughter managed to slam the back door, which instantly locked. I didn't panic at first, for surely I had some old laundry sitting in the garage and could then slip something on and dash to my neighbor's house for help. As luck would have it, I couldn't find one stitch of clothing in that garage; I couldn't even find a towel or old pair of overalls.

I suddenly started to panic, realizing my ten-month-old was in the house naked and the shower was running. I then remembered there was some cloth material in the trunk of my car from an earlier purchase I had made that day. I figured I could get the material, drape it around me, and then dash to the neighbor's house for help. The only problem was this was before cars were made with a pop lock for the trunk. I tore out the back seat and begin tearing the lining to get inside the trunk of the car. I am sure all of this took a few minutes but it seemed like hours. After retrieving the material, I draped it around me like the Statue of Liberty and dashed to my neighbor's house for help. After opening their door and seeing me in such ridiculous condition they fell down laughing.

My neighbor came over with a screw driver, jiggled the lock on the door and it opened instantly. I couldn't believe it! It was that easy. Then I really was frightened. After entering the house I couldn't find my ten-month-old anywhere. The neighbor asked, "Are you sure you had her with you"? I said, of course I'm sure, but after all, I couldn't blame him for asking. After all a woman running around naked is a bit suspect. In a few minutes I found the lost ten-month-old sitting inside the fireplace playing in the ashes. Thankfully nothing really tragic happened, but I am so thankful that I left that material in the trunk of that car.

Kids often provide unexpected challenges and laughter.

Health and aging. Anxiety about the aging process and our health are eased when we can find humor to help us cope with the losses that we experience. As we age, our apprehensions grow and so do the frequency of jokes about our health and aging. Humor about aging will not be nearly as funny to someone in their twenties as someone in their fifties.

☺ The older you get the better you realize you were.
☺ I intend to live forever . . . so far so good.
☺ Old age comes at a bad time.

Some "senior" personal ads seen in Florida newspapers:

☺ Foxy lady: Sexy, fashion-conscious blue-haired beauty, 80s, slim, 5'4" (used to be 5'6"), searching for sharp-looking, sharp-dressing companion. Matching white shoes and belt a plus.

☺ Long-term commitment: Recent widow who has just buried fourth husband, and am looking for someone to round out a six-unit plot. Dizziness, fainting, shortness of breath not a problem.

☺ Serenity now: I am into solitude, long walks, sunrises, the ocean, yoga and meditation. If you are the silent type, let's get together, take our hearing aids out, and enjoy quiet times.

☺ Mint condition: Male, 1932, high mileage, good condition, some hair, many new parts including hip, knee, cornea, valves. Isn't in running condition, but walks well.

Jest for Fun

When watching your favorite TV show, note the gender jokes. Gender differences provide incredible fodder for sitcom material. Numerous classroom projects could be developed through gender joke observations.

Along with the humor about health and aging, weight is a huge societal concern. The popular press constantly bombards us with the dangers of being overweight. A result is that there are numerous jokes about eating. If weight gain is a worry for you, these may seem funny:

☺ Eat right, exercise, die anyway.

☺ If we are what we eat, I'm cheap, fast, and easy.

☺ Health nuts are going to feel stupid someday, lying in the hospital dying of nothing.

Work and Career. Our career choices greatly influence our connections to our humor style. Nurses, police officers, and construction crews all have their own humorous workout styles based on the unique events that occur in their work. There is a special sense of humor that middle school teachers possess that seems foreign to many others. Some say these teachers have been warped after working with hormonal creatures for several years. Maybe the field just attracts a certain humor type.

Anyway, there are certain jokes that middle school teachers find really funny that may be just slightly humorous to the rest of us. Chances are that you share a common humor perspective with those in your field. See if you can determine which employees would appreciate the following:

- ☺ An expert is one who knows more and more about less and less until he knows absolutely everything about nothing.
- ☺ Technology is dominated by those who manage what they do not understand.
- ☺ A meeting is an event at which the minutes are kept and the hours are lost.
- ☺ To err is human, but to really foul things up requires a computer.
- ☺ The primary function of the design engineer is to make things difficult for the fabricator and impossible for the serviceman.
- ☺ Computers are unreliable, but humans are even more unreliable. Any system that depends on human reliability is unreliable.
- ☺ Under the most rigorously controlled conditions of pressure, temperature, volume, humidity, and other variables, the organism will do as it darn well pleases.

 Jest for Fun

Estimate how many times a day you think you laugh out loud. For one day keep a record. How close was your estimate? Do you laugh more now then you did as a child?

2. SEARCH FOR HUMOR TRAINERS AND COACHES

It's important to have the support of others when beginning humor practice. Determine the people in your life who support your optimism and positive energy. Spend increasingly more time with them and limit the time spent with humordoomers. Seek out the funny people in your life and those with whom you laugh. Try a buddy system. Practice your humor with those you trust. Ask your friends to help you with increasing the laughter in your life—most are very willing to do so, as their laughter meter will also escalate.

3. REVIEW YOUR HUMOR WORKOUT FACILITY

Analyze your current environment to see if it can nurture your humor development. The University of Michigan has a web site for positive organization scholarship (www.bus.umich.edu/Positive)—I mention this again because this is a relatively new discipline in the organizational sciences and provides invaluable insights into our own humor practice.

A negative environment can make it difficult, if not impossible, for you to succeed. Sometimes a new workout facility is the answer. (Yes, you might consider a job change). A humorphobic environment with assertive humordoomers will severely limit your humor workout.

There are times when it's not possible to make a job change. Here are a few suggestions for you. Review all possible adaptations you might make within your classroom or work, find one or two others in your building that can support your humergy, and make sure you find stress management techniques to assist you in your life outside of education.

4. SET YOUR HUMOR WORKOUT GOALS

There are several aspects of physical fitness training that create a nice analogy for developing a humor workout. These include:

- ☺ Strength training
- ☺ Flexibility training
- ☺ Aerobics
- ☺ Stress management
- ☺ Cool down

Jest for Fun

Post a large sheet in the staff lounge for celebration of achievement of humor strength training goals. For example, Jody told a joke and actually remembered the punch line. Bob laughed two times this month—up 100 percent over last month.

Strength Training

Strength training will enhance the strength of your own humor style and build on your techniques. Here are some practical techniques.

The ability to laugh at oneself when faced with events beyond one's control, to admit to blunders with humor, and to find humor in all situations is a critical life skill. This skill is one that can be developed at any age; however, since moral and ethical development escalates in the frontal lobe of the preadolescent brain, this seems to be an ideal time to build confidence in one's ability to laugh at mistakes (Sylwester, 2005). This highly developed cognitive ability is a more advanced skill than purposeful clowning and the talent of telling jokes. Since humor proficiency is not universally found in middle school curriculum, many of us would welcome a refresher course.

If you are teaching middle school or have the challenging job of parenting a teenager you have the opportunity to nurture this self-deprecating humor in young folks. Preteen and teenage years are usually a difficult period when most teens laugh at jokes that focus on sex, food, authority figures, and any subject that adults consider off-limits. Humor skill development and acquiring positive emotionality are important in the middle school curriculum. I know! I know these curriculums are maxed out with mandates and "critical" subject matter. Chapter 6 contains numerous ideas for integration of these concepts.

Numerous middle school teachers already use several techniques to model humor for their students. My daughter Rachael is a focused seventh-grade science teacher, but she delights her students with occasional bursts of song and/or otherwise "goofy" behavior. Allowing students to observe your own playfulness will give them the freedom to grow their own humor being.

The search for absurdity and unusual human behavior (especially in oneself) can initiate healthy self-deprecating amusement. Exaggeration and comparison are good ways to begin to laugh at oneself. Even slight exaggeration can tweak your perception of something and take it from difficult to funny. Some examples of self-deprecation include:

☺ *Overstatement.* This is similar to exaggeration in flexibility training but with a focus on oneself; for example, "I used to have an open mind but my brains kept falling out." "I keep pressing the control key but it's not giving me any!" "To save time, let's agree that I know everything." "How about never, is never good for you?" "The face is familiar but I can't quite remember my name." "I took an IQ test and the results were negative."

☺ *Analogy or comparison.* "Elvis is dead and I'm not feeling too good myself." "S/he who laughs last, thinks slowest." "Always remember that you are unique just like everyone else."

There is a difference between being able to poke fun at oneself and the anxious humor that is a result of insecurity. If you feel like a martyr or a victim during this humor workout, the results will not contribute to the positive emotionality and humergy of a healthy humor being.

Self-deprecating humor has long been used by politicians who recognize its ability to acknowledge controversial issues and steal the punch of criticism.

☺ When Ronald Regan's advanced age was used against him during the 1984 campaign, he quipped, "I will not make age an issue in this campaign. I am not going to exploit, for political purposes, my opponent's youth and inexperience."

☺ "To those of you who received honors, awards, and distinctions, I say, well done. And to the 'C' students, I say you too can be president."—George W. Bush accepting an honorary doctorate from his alma mater, Yale University.

☺ "I am Al Gore and I used to be the next president of the United States."—Gore in a speech at Bocconi University in Milan after losing his close race with Bush.

Students might enjoy researching famous folks who were able to poke fun at themselves. Humor seems to be a popular tool with some politicians campaigning for office.

Flexibility Training

Humor practice requires flexibility and the self-confidence to know you will meet the hurdles of life with optimistic amusement. Stretching is a large part of flexibility. One strategy for mental stretching is exaggeration. Stretch the truth. When difficulties occur in your life, take that challenge and use exaggeration to assist in coping. Laughing at the difficulties helps to ease the experience.

"It's been so hot, the trees are whistling for the dogs."

Bending in new ways and stretching your abilities will increase your humor power. Start with an awareness of your emotional state after a review of your baseline data. The optimal goal is to increase your positive energy and strive for the joy-flow stage as described in chapter 2. Our emotional state fluctuates as we continually react to our environment and to our own physical challenges. Life is adapting to change as we strive to find balance and joy in life.

Aerobics

Practice, practice, practice . . .

☺ Look for humor in everything.
☺ Collect humor books, emails, stories, jokes.
☺ Begin with humor that you feel comfortable with and progress to humor that you have not tried before. Send humor via e-mail. Try telling jokes, if you have not done so before, starting with one-liners. Repeat stories that you found funny.
☺ Practice humergy with difficult people in your life. React to them with positive energy and work toward forgiveness.
☺ Play every day.
☺ Have intentional fun. Plan for it.

According to comedian Steve Allen, we can increase our sense of humor by exposing ourselves to humorous life experiences. Search for the everyday humor, because it's all around us. The humor resources such as comedy clubs, light-hearted movies, books, cartoons, and comics are obvious; however, a concerted effort is required to practice the art of exaggeration, to experience silliness, or to choose play. Some people carry props such as puppets or clown noses to wear while trying to spread the humor. This is not a comfort zone of mine, but many find this a creative outlet for humergy. Collecting cartoons, puns, and jokes is a common practice. E-mail has contributed to widespread distribution of comic material. My husband Don delights in receiving and sharing e-jokes. His chuckling lets me know that I will soon be the beneficiary of another joke. I hate to admit it, but when editing this book, I asked him not to send me anymore jokes. I just didn't have time for humor. I guess I needed to reread this chapter, because I usually appreciate the e-jokes sent to me. Sharing humor builds relationships and strengthens trust.

Practice, practice, practice . . .

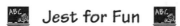

Jest for Fun

Observe humor during the daily newscast. There are numerous examples of humor usage in difficult situations. Peter Jennings when confronted with lung cancer treatment said there would be days when he would be cranky and days when he would be very cranky. Note the exaggeration of his difficult feelings.

Stress Management

As mentioned in chapter 3, humor has been shown to be a stress reliever. The ability to use humor in fear-laden and negative situations reflects an exceptional level of emotional intelligence. Humor can be applied to redirect one's negative energy into a positive form—a highly developed cognitive skill. Recognizing internal frustration and learning to react with humor is beneficial for our health. Our ability to not only survive, but also to thrive in difficult situations is reflected in our humergy techniques.

Eat blueberries and salmon, try bosu, jump rope, dream sweetly, and take care of yourself in all of the recommended ways. These will enhance your sense of humor. Enjoy each morsel of life and laugh during the times when life is hard to swallow. Humor makes the medicine go down in the most amusing way.

Cool Down

Most of us have a preconceived notion of our own sense of humor. For an individual to expand their ability to humergize, it is important to expand an awareness of how to move from the inhibitions of humor toward enjoying humor practice. After you have cooled down, head for the shower. Shower yourself with accolades for completing your humor workout. Now is the time to revisit your goals and set new ones.

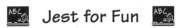

Jest for Fun

If at first you don't succeed, skydiving isn't for you. Be realistic about your workout goals. Don't be afraid to keep trying new things.

5. CHECK YOUR JOY-FLOW STATE

Humor is the vehicle that can help us return to the safety net where learning is fun. Happiness, fun, play, mirth, comedy, joy, and jokes are all terms that have been used to define humor. Humergy is a powerful mind/body connection creating a remarkable feeling of control over one's life. Fully developed characteristics are exhibited by the individual who:

☺ Consistently chooses a positive response pattern in life. The capacity to do this emerges from a focus on creating an affirmative environment (even a mental one) in which to operate.

☺ Welcomes challenge in change, incongruity, and uncertainty. Has the confidence to think outside of the box and see numerous possibilities. If a situation does not progress as planned, another option is found.

☺ Understands that humor is a coping skill that can be a response to change (from small annoyances to a major crisis).

☺ Purposefully uses laughter to ease pain and realizes that laughter is a sign of healing and health.

☺ Uses self-deprecating humor as an exaggerated statement of truth with the knack of laughing at one's own mistakes or difficulties.

☺ Empathizes with other people and is able to "read" the emotions of others. Has the ability to assist others in seeing the humor in difficult situations and elicit laughter in difficult situations. Emotional intelligence operates at full throttle.

☺ Listens to others and honors their feelings. Recognizes that anger in another person usually mirrors fear.

☺ Has the ability to use humor in communicating with others. Highly skilled humergists are able to ease the tension in group meetings by promoting laughter at the situation or at themselves.

☺ Plays frequently and encourages others to do so. Understands that play promotes learning, builds trust, and encourages creativity.

☺ Finds balance in life. Looks at work as a career and the opportunity to expand personal talents and abilities in the service of others.

6. SET NEW HUMOR WORKOUT GOALS

You know the routine. Start over again and practice, practice, practice. . . . (See figure 5-2.)

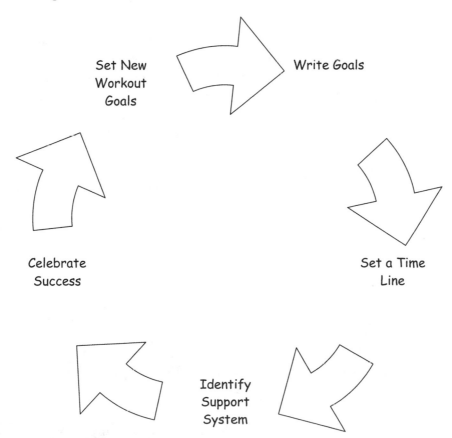

Figure 5-2.   Humor workout cycle.

1. After reviewing appendix 4: Sense of Humor Reflections, write new goals. For example, laugh more often each day, try a new form of play, tell more funny stories, find a supportive colleague, read a funny book, start a school humor mentor program, etc.
2. Set a time line. For example, by the end of the month I will have two coaches in place and will have tried a new form of play each week.
3. Identify your support system. Who have you relied on in the past? Continue the search for colleagues who enjoy humor.
4. Celebrate your success. Be sure to enjoy the success of your humor practice.
5. Set challenging new workout goals. Start over!

Your humor improvement plan will succeed if you initiate a workout time line when you set your goals. Surround yourself with coaches and trainers who will support your humor practice. Celebrate your humor accomplishments. The Humor Styles Inventory will assist you in deciding whether to work your frontal lobes, your laughter lines, your funny bone, or all three. Although both nature and nurture contribute to a sense of humor, humergy is a skill that can be learned and practiced. Encourage others to join you in your quest for optimistic emotionality. Remember that humor is a powerful antidote for stress and will add to your quality of life. Also remember that many playful behaviors have been extinguished from our life and it will take effort and practice to rejuvenate your humor being.

SUMMARY

Everybody can add fun, laughter, and play into their life. Begin with the goal of increasing your humergy level, reducing stress, and bringing your best self to work every day. Your enthusiasm, excitement, and energy are powerful forces that reflect your renewed sense of humor. This humor workout provides benefits that maximize creativity and comprehension by:

   ☺ Increasing the ability to take risks and try new things
   ☺ Expanding the ability to generate ideas

☺ Capturing our attention
☺ Increasing memory storage and retrieval

And facilitate communication with individuals and in groups by:

☺ Enabling observation of our internal emotional state
☺ Reflecting the inner spirit of self and others
☺ Increasing the ability to "read" the emotions of others
☺ Reducing tension, fear and anger
☺ Nurturing trust
☺ Increasing group energy and positive group dynamics

Your individual humor workout will enhance your life and bring laughter, fun, and joy, both to you and to all around you.

Powerful Practice—Strategies for School Leaders

Focus on your own sense of humor:

☺ Review the developmental stages of humor in the previous chapter of this book. Reflect on your own humor history.
☺ Take the Humor Styles Inventory found in appendix 5. Practice the skills that strengthen the humor style you enjoy. Try different forms of humor at a pace of one a month. Note the reaction of your colleagues.
☺ Choose a certain time each day to record or journal the times that you laughed. Try to increase your humor stats—frequency, quality of humor recorded.
☺ Observe the humor of those people in your life that make you jump with joy and who fill your life with humergy. Seek out those individuals and create some zest together.
☺ Make it a goal in your life to make everyone that you come into contact with laugh or at least smile. Sometimes it is easiest to practice with people you do not know, such as people in the checkout line or in the elevator, clerks, wait staff, or toll booth attendants.

Play every day. Encourage your colleagues in the art of play.

☺ Go to the park and swing (you can be a swinger too).
☺ Get out your hula-hoop and see if you can still make it go up and down your body—okay, just around the waist!
☺ Find your old yo-yo. Walk the dog or go around the world.
☺ Dance and shout to your favorite music.
☺ Sing loudly in the car, shower, or—if you're talented—in public.
☺ Do the Twist, the Mashed Potato, a country line dance.
☺ Try something new that's a stretch for you—bungee jumping (pun intended), board games, sports, and artistic endeavors.
☺ Get on your neighbor's pogo stick.
☺ Build a tree house and spend time there making funny monkey noises.
☺ Play with Lincoln Logs or Tinker Toys.
☺ Pitch a tent in your back yard. Invite someone over for tent talk.
☺ Teach the kids in your neighborhood how to play Kick the Can.
☺ Experiment with string, kites, magnets, Silly Putty, and bubbles.
☺ Find old toys at garage sales and reminisce. Share the joys of these toys with anyone who will play with them too.

Note: if you do not know what some of these "play" items refer to, ask your fellow "seasoned" teachers.

Jest for Fun

Sponsor an "It Takes Balls to Relieve Stress" activity. Give each staff member a different ball (football, baseball, golf ball, bowling, etc.). This person pairs with another to brainstorm ways the ball can be used to relieve stress. Each week a different ball activity can be initiated by those staff.

Study Group Focus

☺ Take the Humor Styles Inventory (appendix 5). Use the Categories of Humor (appendix 6) and Fun Websites (bibliography) resources. Share your results with the group. Discuss how different humor styles affect communication between colleagues. Small groups of those with similar styles would be intriguing.

☺ Use your study group as a support system for increasing the humor in your lives. Share humor resources. Do your humor workout together.

☺ Choose books on humor (see bibliography) to read as a book club format. Generate discussions on the book content with different members serving as facilitators.

☺ Compile a humor "recipe" book as a fundraising effort. Use the money to increase your humor library or to send teachers to a humor conference.

☺ Form a Laughter Club; information can be received from Steve Wilson, founder, president, and cheerman of The Bored(tm) World Laughter Tour, Inc. (www.WorldLaughterTour.com).

Café Conversations

Review current literature on the importance of humor and stress management. How do we already support the humor practice of teachers in our school environment? Identify the teachers who exhibit exemplary humor practice. How can the talents of these educators be maximized in our school culture? How can we increase support for a wellness lifestyle that includes humor workouts?

"I was going to buy a copy of *The Power of Positive Thinking*. Then I wondered what the heck kind of good that would do."

Chapter 6

HUMOR EXTRAVAGANZA

It's a Circus out There!

"It's kind of fun to do the impossible." —Walt Disney

The activities compiled in this chapter have been collected from educators by the "search and steal" methodology. They have been gathered from educators at workshops I have conducted, from classroom visits, and by generally doing the one thing that we do best—taking a creative idea and adapting it for individual classroom use.

Many readers may find it difficult to actually implement some of the strategies found in this book. I have been continuously amazed at how difficult it is to use fun, laughter, and humor in our educational systems. Is there an unspoken rule that having fun is forbidden in schools? What is it we are afraid of? The higher the grade level, the more difficult it is to implement humor practice. Some of the more adventuresome high school teachers use cartoons and puns. Anything else is dismissed as too elementary or childish to be considered. Your stories continue to reinforce my belief that humor and fun are like many of our wild animals—in danger of becoming extinct in our schools. These are a few actual conversations I have encountered.

A high school teacher reviewed some of these ideas and cautioned me, "we're not supposed to have parties, although some teachers secretly do. In our school system the clowning and parties need to be kept at the elementary levels."

When a teacher that I know was moving to second grade after teaching kindergarten for several years, the principal came to her and declared: "now you won't be able to sing anymore." She got the message that there was no time for fun and games in second grade. Teaching was a serious business.

A teacher with a brain-compatible classroom had children actively engaged in a variety of activities. They were, of course, talking and sharing ideas. The principal came in and implied her room was too noisy when she said, "there's not one kid talking next door!" Numerous teachers allege that all they can accomplish during the school day is preparation and testing for state and federal mandates. Many are saddened by the fact that there is no time for fun. One teacher tried some creative activities with her fifth grade students and the students admonished her for having too much fun. Another teacher said there is bitterness among the teachers at her school because of all they are already expected to do. Humor would be adding just one more thing to the already overworked staff.

High school teachers have indicated that some of these ideas are childish, too difficult to implement, or that they are not just willing to put forth the effort to try something this risky without a guarantee of higher test scores. A principal disclosed that he believed in using humor, but was afraid that the perception from the community would be that students were "not working." As mentioned previously, I have been overwhelmed by the number of teachers who have reported that they can only have fun after they close the classroom door. Many told me that they do this frequently, because they worry that others might misinterpret the laughter coming from their rooms. They actually try to suppress the laughter or keep it to a minimum because of these fears.

Whew! Convincing educators that humor is important is not an issue. Most teachers will readily tell me that they value humor. However, persuading educators to actually implement humor practice is a challenge. It seems that by fourth grade, even some of the students have become reluctant to have fun in school. A fourth grade teacher confided that she was integrating humor and a student told her he was too old for that kind of stuff. Humorphobia or fear of humor as described in chapter 4 does permeate our educational system.

The fact remains: *humor does facilitate learning.* However, because of the prevalence of humorphobia in our schools, it's imperative that you clearly understand and articulate your goals when initiating humor. Please feel free to incorporate these research-based rationales for why humor can and should be integrated into your classroom. Review the research in chapter 3 that identified the following advantages for using humor:

- ☺ Captures and retains student attention
- ☺ Expands student comprehension
- ☺ Increases the opportunity for memory retention
- ☺ Builds relationships with students and colleagues
- ☺ Creates a nurturing environment for learning
- ☺ Supports classroom management
- ☺ Helps people cope
- ☺ Enhances the joyful craft of teaching and learning

Don't be discouraged if your initial attempt at integrating humor feels strange or doesn't go very well. As mentioned throughout this book, our school cultures generally don't encourage humor initiation and practice. In fact, you may fear being reprimanded for having fun. In spite of these obstacles, your school culture might limit the feasibility of trying some of these ideas. For instance, if there is a rule against parties, you won't be able to try the party ideas this year. However, I strongly encourage you to try on your humor persona, be a little daring, and have some fun.

Educators often operate in an atmosphere that feels like a three-ring circus (see figure 6-1). Remember most of these search and steal methods can be adapted for any classroom. Let your imagination go wild as you review the activities in all three rings.

Ring One: Grade Level Performance
Ring Two: Subject Level Stunts
Ring Three: Instructional Innovations: The Educator's Tackle Box

Ring # 2

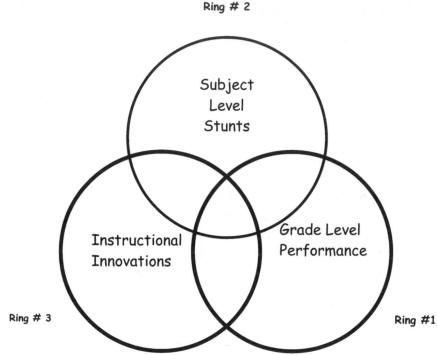

Ring # 3   Ring #1

Figure 6-1.   Three-ring circus.

 Jest for Fun

At the first in-service of the school year, have participants complete the following sentence: "Being an educator in this school is like being in a circus because . . ." These can be posted and referred to whenever challenges occur during the school year.

RING ONE: GRADE LEVEL PERFORMANCE

Put these tricks in your bag and pull them out when you want to stimulate, excite, and grab attention. Let the magic of humor get your creative juices flowing. While these are designed for the specific stages of humor development (as described in chapter 2), most can be adapted for any age.

Knock-Knock Exploits (Grades Pre-K–3)

☺ Put a different riddle on the bulletin board each day, with sheets of paper and a box below. Students can guess the answer and put the sheet with their name on it in the box. Teachers can acknowledge the correct answers the next day with silly prizes or just a posted list of those who answered correctly.

☺ The "funny corner" encourages clowning creativity. Provide a small desk area with a mirror and clown props. Students can choose to become a colorful character in history (related to your content area). Drama and storytelling can be integrated as a way to make characters come alive.

☺ Joke and riddle books excite even the bored child. Make sure that there are numerous opportunities to explore books that encourage humor.

☺ Finger puppets generate ways to review material. Help students focus by using the puppets to point to the reading material with their puppet finger. (Finger puppets are easily made with a fine point marker and putting a face on the finger tip.)

☺ Rhythm and rhyme are more fun with a Dr. Seuss theme. Have a Cat in the Hat Day or serve green eggs and ham. Use this format to introduce rhymes. Adapting Dr. Seuss to particular lesson plans has been a successful strategy implemented by numerous teachers at all grade levels.

Riddle-De-Dee Festival (Grades 3–5)

☺ Begin each day with a riddle or funny story chosen by one of the students. An interesting assignment is to have the students create a riddle about their lesson. The class can brainstorm the answer.

☺ One day a week the principal can invite a student to read a riddle over the loudspeaker. Students can write their answers and drop them in the riddle box in each room. The principal posts the names of the students who got the correct answer. The student who figures out the most riddles by the end of the month gets to select or create a riddle for the school newsletter.

☺ Use familiar songs and change the words to include facts that need to be remembered (see appendix 9: Familiar Song List).

Pun-Fun Spectacular (Grades 6–8)

☺ Greet students with secret visual signals that give them a clue about the lesson for the day—any goofy move will do. Refer to the signal when they leave as a reminder of the key point you want them to remember. Remember, movement helps plant information into the long term memory. A study of the cells could initiate a "cell" phone conversation. A choking sign could mean that they must learn one important concept or "choke" on the test. Three fingers in the air might indicate the three vital things they need to learn that day.

☺ Have a backwards day. Everything is backwards. Clothing can be worn backwards or start the day with whatever rituals you usually end the day with. Take any list or sequential information the students are learning and have them recite it backwards. This works well with spelling words.

☺ Encourage puns. Give extra credit for any puns that relate to the material that you are studying.

☺ Wrap a present. Set it on your desk. Give clues as to what is inside. It can be the title of the book you will be reading, the name of your next science unit, or the summary of the material you have been working on. Whoever figures out what's in the box gets to open the present and read the information to the class.

Joy-Flow Entertainment (High School to adult)

☺ Check out the previous activities. You may be able to adapt one of them for your class.

☺ Have students share the best "hooks" used by their previous teachers. What humor helped them to remember the information they needed to learn? How can they use this information to help them learn in your class?

☺ Have students create their own bumper sticker, e-mail addresses, or license plates highlighting an aspect of a lesson.

☺ Party. Let students plan the food, games, and activities as a culmination of a lesson or as a reward for working hard. Several times of the year adapt to a party theme; for example, "Exam day party: Celebrate what you know!" "First day of spring party," "Monthly birthday party," "Groundhog Day party," or "Chinese New Year."

☺ Create contests, games, or events with the purpose of sinking information into the long-term memory.

☺ Hat day (if you're able to bend dress rules for one day). Students choose a hat that links to the content they need to remember. They tell their hat story and link the information to the current lesson.

☺ Kite-flying contest. Students create a kite that contains the information they need to remember for the lesson. The kites can be hung around the room to remind them of this information. When all students have mastered all of the information, they get to fly the kites. You can tell them to "go fly a kite!"

☺ Jump rope contest. Students create the jingles for jumping that reflect the content of the lessons. Have students try the jingles with individual jump ropes or with the old method of two kids holding the ends while others jump. Clean rap or hip-hop rhymes might be included.

☺ Club or organization activity. Have a Last Comedian Standing contest based on the television program. (Material needs to be preapproved by advisor.) Admission to this event would be a bar of soap or package of toilet paper for the local homeless shelter or cans of food for the food pantry. (Contact the shelter to see what they need.)

☺ Find cartoons that highlight the lesson. You might start with one or two and add to your collection each year. Coordinate with other staff members to supplement these collections by having each teacher collect a cartoon for different lessons and sharing.

☺ Student writing assignment possibilities: Is there a perceived need to use and abuse drugs as a crutch or excuse for being silly? What are the connections between fun and learning? How does one distinguish between appropriate and inappropriate humor? Do students have the right to experience fun, silliness, and humor while in school? Explore the use of toys and adaptation for the curriculum (see appendix 10: Toy List).

RING TWO: SUBJECT LEVEL STUNTS

Incredible and amazing feats of humor in each of the content areas will be fun to try. Get a colleague to collaborate with you and encourage each other in your quest for expanding the humor in your classrooms.

Art

"Everyone has a photographic memory. Some, like me, just don't have any film."

Creative cartooning. Ask students to draw cartoons that are linked to their current history studies or to current events.

Fashion clown masks. Have students develop their own unique clown persona. Clown masks can also be created to depict a famous character from history or literature. These can be worn when giving a presentation about their character.

Drama/Speech

"What would Scooby Doo?"

☺ Sponsor a "Last Comedian Standing" contest.
☺ Start an improvisational theater group.
☺ Study and practice timing for jokes and stories.
☺ Watch episodes of *Whose Line Is It Anyway?* Adapt your own classroom version and perform for the PTA, school board, or as a fund-raiser. Be sure to preview the episodes for appropriate humor.

Health

"Health nuts are going to feel stupid someday, lying in hospitals dying of nothing."

☺ Have students research the health benefits of laughter. Explore the myths and facts about humor and laughter.
☺ Assign a project on the effects of positive psychology and the implications for learning.

☺ Analyze the relationship between stress, learning, and humor.
☺ Study the research on humor and brain imaging. Where is humor located in the brain?

Foreign Languages

"If you look like your passport, you probably need the trip."

☺ Practice telling jokes and stories in different languages.
☺ Identify how a joke changes in translation.
☺ Review the humor from various countries. Compare the differences in cultural humor.

Math

"Ratio of an igloo's circumference to its diameter = Eskimo Pi"

☺ Use rhythm and rhyme to memorize formulas.
☺ Add humor to story problems by changing some words to silly examples (for example, pop stars). Use funny stories as the initial basis for the story problems.
☺ Have a Mirthful Math Day with students taking turns telling jokes after each set of problems.
☺ Watch a variety of comedians (clean humor, of course) and calculate the time between the punch line and the laughter impact. Discuss the implications that timing has on humor. This can be the basis for a bar graph. Have students tell one joke to different groups with different timing lapses. Graph the laughter response.
☺ Have each student keep track of how often they laugh. Chart the numbers according to times of day, who they were with, etc. Use as a graphing assignment.
☺ Let students answer math problems with the number of their favorite sports hero. For instance the answer for number 23 would be Michael Jordon. Have them do problems with Michael Jordon and current star athlete numbers. Encourage them to create problems for each other using this method. This is a good hook for some students who are not too interested in math, but love sports.

Music

> "I found myself utterly depressed the other day and spent the entire afternoon listening to Celine Dion records . . . at least that's what I thought I was doing. Turns out the cat had just fallen into the dryer and was trying to get out."
>
> —Julian Clary

☺ Review some of the music used in comedy films. Compare with the music used in romantic scores, horror movies, adventure cartoons, etc. What are the differences?

☺ Research instruments used as a part of a circus or comedy performance. How were the instruments integrated into routines? For example, Blue Man Group, late night talk shows. Note how drums and cymbals are often used to highlight the end of a joke.

☺ Have a kazoo play day.

☺ Study the different pitches and sounds of laughter.

☺ Find musical scores that elicit laughter as an integral part of the piece.

Physical Education and Sports

> "Marathon runners with bad footwear suffer the agony of defeat."

☺ Try laughter for an initial stretching exercise. Practice a variety of laughs, giggles, belly laughs, with laughter eventually shaking every body part. Discuss why laughter is healthy. Does it really increase the flow of oxygen to every part of the body?

☺ Review the Three Stooges, *I Love Lucy*, and Charlie Chaplin. Discuss the physical requirements of slapstick. Practice a safe slapstick comedy move or routine.

☺ Use laughter as a relaxation technique before competitive events. It will boggle the competitor's minds to hear your team laughing out loud before the performance. Use laughter as your secret weapon. (Remind students that laughing at someone is inappropriate and can be considered bullying behavior.)

Reading

"Experience is a wonderful thing; it enables you to recognize a mistake when you make it again."

☺ Have each student bring in a joke, pun, or riddle (grade 5–12 teachers may need to review for appropriate material). After a discussion to analyze the humor, students can read additional material analyzing how word play and language variances can generate humor.

☺ Read a funny story out loud every day. Ask students if they found the material funny. Initiate a discussion of humor styles (see appendix 5). This is a good discussion starter on the nuances of language usage, speech, and timing.

☺ Initiate a directory of funny/humorous books read by the students. Keep adding to the list. Post this list to share with others and create a blog to discuss the books. Have a contest with other classes to see who can generate the longest list.

☺ Use cartoon bubbles as story starters. Have students bring cartoons to class to share. Let them try their skills at using the visual aid of a cartoon as a writing prompt.

☺ Research and read about the different styles of comedy: clowning, pantomime, improv, impressionist, master of ceremonies, magician, stand-up comic.

☺ Research the difference in writing style of a comedy or tragedy. Look at Shakespeare's tragedy and comedy works. Compare and contrast.

Science

"Two hydrogen atoms walk into a bar. One says, 'I've lost my electron.' The other says, 'Are you sure?' The first replies, 'Yes, I'm positive.'"

☺ Research if the above joke is true or false and why.

☺ Research humor (the humor glossary in appendix 8 can be a starting point).

☺ Where is humor located in the brain?

☺ What happens when we laugh?

☺ Explore the relationship between facial expressions and our emotions. Conduct experiments analyzing emotional reactions. How do police tell if someone is lying or telling the truth?

☺ Conduct laughter research. Have the students do a survey on laughter. Chart the numbers. Collect data on the time of day that there was the most laughter.

☺ Assign a research study on play therapy, humor therapy, and/or the relationship between laughter and stress.

☺ Study the science of roller coasters, Ferris wheels, and video games. Do people laugh during these rides? Does fear generate laughter? What evokes the emotions evident at amusement parks?

☺ Study the humor of animals.

☺ Do dogs have a sense of humor?

☺ What sounds do monkeys make to express amusement? Is it different than humans?

Social Studies

"Suppose you were an idiot and suppose you were a member of Congress . . . but I repeat myself."
—Mark Twain

☺ Initiate a study of the humor during a historical period in time. Would this humor be considered funny today? Ben Franklin's works are a delightful source of material. Include the work of Shakespeare, Mark Twain, Will Rogers, and Aristotle.

☺ Initiate a treasure hunt to stimulate interest in geographic locations. Students choose a location and create clues to assist classmates in locating various points. These clues can be riddles or cartoons.

☺ Research the humor of a variety of historical periods. What role did jesters play? Why do we identify works of Shakespeare as comedy or tragedy?

☺ Examine the cartoons of different periods in American history and discuss the intended message about the political climate of that era.

☺ Political cartoons depict social viewpoints. Have students bring cartoons to class and discuss the message these cartoons portray.

☺ Creative cartooning is a great way for students to depict the period of history currently being reviewed.

☺ Cultural differences are evident in humor usage. Find jokes that are universal in nature and cut across cultural and ethnic differences.

☺ Students can write to their favorite cartoonist asking her to share how she became interested in political cartooning.

☺ Create a wax museum with students dressing as a famous historical character. They have a button on their wrist that turns them on so they can speak about their contribution to history. This is a great event for parent night.

Writing

"I may be schizophrenic but at least I have each other."

☺ Students choose the college they think they would like to attend. They research the school mascot and write about how it was chosen, how the mascot performs, and how it reflects the school culture. Discuss why schools have mascots.

☺ Blow them away. Put a prompt inside a balloon. Each student blows up their balloon and pops it to find the story prompt. Can use the silly word list in appendix 11.

☺ Bring in Chinese fortune cookies. Use these sayings as story starters. Have students create fortunes for each other.

☺ Cartoon clues. Use unidentified cartoons as story prompts.

☺ Non-sense: Provide a list of nonsense words that students can choose to be included in their writing or poetry assignment. Can use silly word list in appendix 11.

☺ Dr. Seuss revisited. Have *And to Think That I Saw It on Mulberry Street* week. Apply the Seuss format as a creative writing technique. Dramatize parts of the Seuss book and have students manipulate the conclusion using a current unit of study.

☺ Unmasking our creativity. For descriptive writing, each student can create a clown persona and then dress up as that clown and provide a short skit revealing the personality behind the "mask."

☺ Story exchange. Have each student write the beginning of a story and exchange with another student to finish the story.

☺ Hot potato writing. Students begin by sitting in a circle. Each student writes, addressing the topic chosen from your current curriculum content. When the music starts, each student passes the paper to the right until the music stops. They then read what is written and continue that story. When the music starts the passing begins again. This can continue for several passes. These stories are funny when read aloud. Students can then edit the stories in small groups.

☺ Drawing to music. Student choice of an appropriate music selection begins with students drawing in time to the music. Music is played in short segments. When the music stops, each student folds their paper in two and papers are passed around until the music stops. This can be repeated, reversing the passing order. The picture that they receive is their story starter. Using their imagination, they write about what they visualize on the paper. Papers can be returned to the original artist for story completion.

☺ Topic comedy. Create a comedy bulletin board and post humorous writings created by the students or appropriate humorous stories they have found. A theme can be used, such as lightbulb jokes, "Why did the chicken cross the road?" jokes, or true stories. All material is reviewed by the teacher before posting.

☺ Color me funny. Discuss the innovative ideas generated by a color, such as Blue Man Group, the Blues Brothers, and *Blue's Clues*. Red can be used for a Valentine's Day theme with topics such as the Red Sea, the Red Hot Chili Peppers, the Red Cross, and the Red Hat Society. Choose a color and have the class come up with as many topics around that color as possible. Write about how color can color creative thinking.

☺ As part of a lesson combining humor style and writing, pass out clown noses and/or a variety of hats and give the students a choice to wear them to see how it impacts their writing. The purpose is to alter their viewpoint. Discuss how they felt as part of this experiment. There will be different comfort levels with varying insights into humor styles.

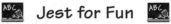

Jest for Fun

Discuss this quote by Nicholas Cage with your students: "Classes were always a bore to me. I wanted to learn things on my own, not by presentations. I was a loudmouth and a clown. It came as a surprise to me, later, that I could be serious and still get attention."

RING THREE: INSTRUCTIONAL INNOVATIONS AND THE EDUCATOR'S TACKLE BOX

As a review of chapter 3, teachers have the opportunity to use humor as a valued tool in their educator's tackle box. In order to maximize learning, educators can use humor to increase understanding and strengthen the possibility that information will be stored in long-term memory. These research-based instructional strategies are an invaluable resource for the educator's tackle box. Here is a recap of the hook, line, and sinker strategy for integrating humor in the curriculum.

1. Capture and retain student attention: The hook
2. Expand student comprehension: The Line—practice and repetition
3. Increase the opportunity for memory retention: The sinker—feedback and reflection

Hook them with advance organizers:

☺ Use different humorous themes to help students get excited about the upcoming unit of study.
☺ Circus themes are adaptable for almost any topic and provide lots of possibilities for graphic organizers. (This chapter is an example.) There are numerous additional thematic units that creative teachers enjoy using that employ humor as a hook.
☺ Employ popular animated movies as the basis for planning. *Shrek*, *Finding Nemo*, *Antz*, and Mickey Mouse are great possibilities.
☺ Adapt David Letterman's top ten list of what will be learned or why they will like this lesson.

Hook them with visuals, story maps, word walls, jigsaws, pair/share, and change of state activities:

☺ Cartoons can be used to depict everything from spelling words to political concepts. They are great story starters, and can be used for word walls and jigsaws.
☺ Pair/share: Student #1 puts on a clown nose and begins talking nonstop to student #2 for five minutes about everything learned on a specific topic. Then student #2 puts on the nose and talks

nonstop for five minutes without repeating any material. Switch pairs and repeat activity.

☺ Identify key information you want students to remember. Print each topic on different large clown shoes. Laminate the paper shoes and tape on the floor around your room. Have enough for each student. Each student starts on a shoe. Play music. When the music stops the students read the information on their shoe. When the music begins, they walk from shoe to shoe until the music stops. They again read the information. Track one student so you are sure everyone gets to read every piece of information. When they are back at their seats, review and see if they remember which shoe the information was on and how much they remembered.

☺ Remember, brains fall asleep after ten to fifteen minutes of lull. Plan a change of state to regain attention every so often.

☺ Encourage the use of humor in completing assignments. Give extra credit for humor that supports the content and is integrated into homework.

☺ Kazoos can be used for memorization. The class can do a type of choral reading on kazoos—repeating the piece together. (This takes an especially hardy teacher.)

☺ As a review technique, use the improvisation format of *Whose Line Is It Anyway?* Have students write the review prompt and two to three students perform the improvisation while the others guess the key learning component.

☺ Encourage students to adapt review information to their favorite music. Student can work in small study groups to accomplish this as part of a homework assignment. (Music must be appropriate!)

The *line* of cooperative learning:

☺ Have students write test questions on small pieces of paper. Have each student insert these into balloons and blow up balloons. A balloon volleyball format can be used, with the team earning the right to answer the question inside the balloon if they win the set. When the balloon is popped, the team must answer the question inside of their balloon to score a point. This can be an ongoing game spanning several days and used as a break time activity.

☺ Give each group a different set of toys (for example, slinkies, yo-yos, pickup sticks, puppets, legos). These props can be used to create an analogy for the material you are studying. For example, "the balance of powers in the United States Government is like a yo-yo because . . ." They can also be used to simulate discussion between two opposing viewpoints using the puppets.

Sinker (feedback):

☺ Affirm any attempts at appropriate humor from your students, especially humor that reinforces a lesson. Provide resources and prizes for successful humor efforts that are linked to learning.

☺ Have students take the Humor Styles Inventory. Have each student fill out a sheet with their name at the top and listing their favorite comedian and joke. Leave space at the bottom for other students/staff to post comments on why they appreciate the humor of this student. Encourage students to notice the humor of their classmates.

Sinker (reflection):

☺ Comedian biography. Students choose their favorite comedian and write a biography about their lives. This can provide a springboard for a discussion of humor styles and how it impacts learning and communication. How is humor related to communication? How did this comedian succeed in communicating?

☺ Students create memory hooks for their current lesson using silly rhymes or cartoons. Have students share their memory hook with the class.

☺ Use a clown happy face handout as a reflection technique after the lesson. Each of the face parts represents a different aspect of learning. The eyes depict what the student saw. The mouth is what they would like to tell others about the lesson. The nose can link what students found funny about the material. The ears are what the student heard the teacher tell about the lesson.

Sinker (assessment):

☺ Each student creates a test question using a riddle format. (This can be a homework assignment.) Each student shares their riddle with the class before the assessment is given. These riddles can be incorporated into the actual assessment. (For example, who was the Queen of Denial/the Nile.)

☺ Add a funny test question in the middle of the assessment. For example, who is your favorite teacher right at this moment? Acknowledge everyone who writes in your name.

☺ Have a bulletin board titled: This Clown Nose (knows). Students write questions/reflections on red circle noses that are put in the middle of the clown faces they created.

☺ Provide cartoons without captions and have students use a cartoon format to summarize different ideas from the lesson. Save the best ones from year to year and use them to introduce lessons or at various times to reinforce learning.

THE RINGMASTER: CLASSROOM MANAGEMENT MAGIC

The most important trick in classroom management is having the students actively engaged in their own learning. Step right up to see the tricks of humor used to tame the lions and tigers. Watch as the class clowns perform amazing feats right before your very eyes. Boredom and discipline problems disappear as you create the magic of fun in learning. The brain-compatible classroom usually doesn't have too many discipline issues. If students are having fun, the chances for inappropriate behavior decrease. Here are some tricks to ensure engaged learning is taking place.

Embrace Play for Discovery-based Learning

☺ Have a variety of toys and games available (see the suggested list in appendix 10). Apply the rule that anything can be used as long as it does not distract another student's learning process.

☺ Provide an area in your room for play activities. Change the materials frequently to encourage creativity.

☺ Constantly look for opportunities to play. Give the students free play time. This time can be used to write, read, role-play, dream, and just think! Set up play centers in the room to promote play.

Offer Choice: Encourage Students to Shape Their Own Learning

☺ Allow the students to sit, lounge, or stand as they learn. Desks can cramp the brain and humor. If students must be at their desk, make the rule that one part of their body must be touching their desk at all times.

☺ When consequences are necessary, give choices: you can choose to write a thoughtful letter of apology or clean the desktop of every student in the classroom after school.

☺ Create humor lifelines for times of stress. Phone a friend (can use cell phones if school guidelines allow it). Write a friend for advice. Maybe a humor advice column can be created in the school newsletter with students writing for advice.

☺ Review brain-based learning research for providing student choice, including Eric Jensen's *Teaching with the Brain in Mind* (1998) and Kathy Nunley's *Layered Curriculum* (2001). (More information can be found at help4teachers.com.)

☺ Include extra credit for humor usage in any writing assignment.

Incorporate Movement and the Arts to Stimulate Cognitive Growth

☺ Provide a *change of state* every ten to fifteen minutes (figure 6-2). The brain goes to sleep after about ten minutes of inertia (and listening to the sound of a teacher's voice can induce sleep in less time!).

☺ Use humorobics, the practice of laughter to oxygenize the brain. Several minutes of hearty laughter is great exercise and a lot of fun. Steve Wilson's Laughter Clubs provide numerous ideas for encouraging laughter.

☺ Integrate art and music whenever possible.

☺ Encourage activities that get kids moving.

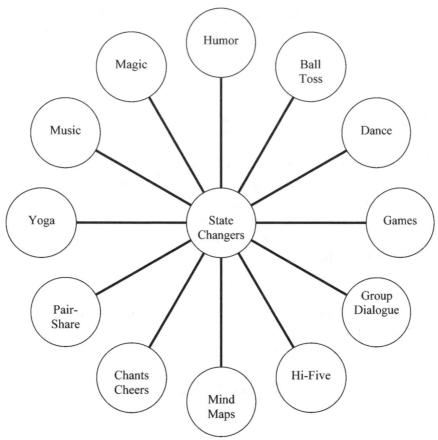

Figure 6-2. State changer ideas.

Integrate Discipline to Provide Safety and Security for Joyful Learning

Mark Goor (1989) views humor as an alternative to authoritarian discipline. He notes that humor emerges when teachers connect personally with the students through humor.

☺ Laughter banishes most anger and fear. Use exaggeration and gentle teasing to prevent discipline problems. This is an art not a science. Observe compassionate, seasoned teachers who are known for their sense of humor and fun. Ask them for their strategies.

☺ Honor the class clown and all students in their "funny" efforts. Ask clowns to find humor during the difficult times. "How can we find something good about this?" Or "Who can find something funny about this?"" Is there anyone who can find some humor in this situation?"

☺ Pair the class clown with an overanxious student. (This may not always work but deserves an attempt to provide a balance for both of them.)

☺ Support an all-school class clown contest. (This could be done in individual classrooms, with the winner qualifying to compete in the all-school contest.) Give prizes for the most positive upbeat clowning.

☺ Use student humor to support the rules and regulations.

☺ Create spoonerisms (transposing initial letters) for the class rules: Te on Bime or Tait your Wurn.

☺ Have students create a song or quote about rules: "Be on time for class—if you want to pass." "Go 4 it @ your school library." "It's the real thing—studying!"

☺ Challenge students to find historical consequences for poor choices (for example, dunce hat, sitting in the corner, writing phrases one hundred times). Discuss alternatives that would be effective with students today (for example, no cell phone for two days).

☺ Encourage students to read funny stories about famous people who had difficulty in school and make a list of why and how these students succeeded.

Encourage Positive Clowning Practice

Class clowns have traditionally been feared as a cause of disruption. A courageous teacher skillfully uses the strong emotions of the clown as a benefit for the classroom.

☺ Take turns telling jokes and funny stories.
☺ Share spoonerisms.
☺ Discover the art of exaggeration.
☺ Practice timing.
☺ Study the power of repetitions.

☺ Practice pantomime.

☺ Research clowning as an art and science.

Provide Humor Resources

☺ Expand your humor library. Be sure there are lots of joke books and literary books that are specifically designated for fun.

☺ Kids love to be in charge of observing the humor in your class. Keeping a class journal of laughter is a good idea and can be reviewed often to remind the class of the fun they had.

☺ Have a humor club. Share online resources. See the bibliography for a list of websites.

☺ Increase the fun in your own life. The more fun you are having, the more you will enjoy teaching, and the more your students will benefit.

IF IT IS FUN, IT WILL GET DONE!

It is almost impossible for the educator to keep track of all of the activities going on in a brain-based classroom with the clowns, mice, fish, tigers, squirrels, elephants, and talented learners performing amazing acts. The ringmaster literally must have eyes in the back of her head and be able to balance and coordinate the activities in all three rings. Interruptions and the unexpected are part of each day. Successful ringmasters are leaders with courage, passion, and the ability to enjoy the wild side of learning. An educator's belief system impacts every teaching decision that is made in each of the areas of the framework.

The interdisciplinary nature of humor is an advantage for encouraging creativity. The University of Michigan in 1992 actually designated spring as the comedy semester. Over six hundred students enrolled in humor-related courses. Humor lends itself to a schoolwide focus on learning through fun.

Having fun creates a healthy learning environment. Having fun energizes both teachers and students. Having fun promotes a sense of humor and produces positive emotionality. The circus is coming. Humor is your ticket to enjoy life under the big top where learning is *fun*damental.

Jest for Fun

Have an all-school circus parade, with each class representing a value important in character education. This could be used during homecoming week, with a circus theme used to emphasize positive life choices. Examples might be tiger trainers that exhibit courage and trapeze artists that demonstrate flexibility. Cirque du Soleil could be used as an additional example of a creative circus theme.

SUMMARY

Making the most of the creativity of students will reinforce the ideas that you want planted in permanent memory. Jokes, icebreakers, and improvisational comedy are just a few of the techniques that can be integrated to maximize linking fun with learning. Using humor to support learning is a purposeful, challenging, and splendid responsibility. Once there is a comfort level with expanding your use of humor, there will be an increasing energy for learning and lots of fun in your classroom. Here are some tricks of the trade that can be included under your big top:

Ring one. Grade level tricks
Ring two. Subject level stunts and multidisciplinary strategies
Ring three. Specific cognitive strategies for using humor to increase student achievement
Ringmaster. Tricks of behavior management

The ideas in this chapter have been adapted from creative educators who were eager to share classroom applications and personal examples of humor in action. These educators use humor to create a joyful environment for learning, where humor is not only valued, but an integral component of student learning. An abundance of resources can be used to jump-start the engine of humor power and are absolutely free for teachers who have the courage to take the humor challenge.

Powerful Practice—Strategies for School Leaders

☺ Have a schoolwide circus theme. Promote clowning and fun. Brainstorm ways that your school is like a circus. Encourage the students to become involved in organizing activities around this theme to match the content of their learning. (Other energizing themes can be used—Disney, magic, Kermit the frog, blues group.) Promote the concept that school is fun, learning is fun, etc. At the middle school and high school levels, encourage students to choose the theme.

☺ Manage behavior by using humor. Make observations of teachers who effectively use humor to discipline challenging students. Have these teachers serve as mentors for novice teachers or others who would like to improve their classroom management techniques. Have a staff session to brainstorm creative clowning and find ideas to effectively channel the energy of the class clown. Initiate laughter practice, in which you observe and record the impact of formal laughter practice on student behavior.

☺ Write with humor across the curriculum. Plan and study techniques for integrating humor in the writing process on a school-wide basis. Publish a special humor newsletter featuring student writing. Pick a school comedian or mascot after schoolwide research into personalities and humor of favorite humorists. Each class could research a humorist, write a script, and do a comic presentation featuring the humor style of the comedian. There could be a school vote on the selection of the humor style with a celebration of humor at various school events. A great theme for pep assemblies, parent/teacher conferences, testing week, etc. Contact the local media to do a feature on what students have written about their favorite comedian. Invite that comedian to the school!

☺ Bumper sticker bombardment. Study the language usage of bumper stickers to convey a message. Create your own bumper stickers as indicated by your school programs or goals (see appendix 12).

Remember, the goal in this chapter is to expand your use of humor to hook student attention and to link humor to the lesson for maximum comprehension and retention. Humor is also important for creating a stress-free environment to optimize learning.

Study Group Focus

☺ Gather data on the current use of humor across the curriculum and the implications for the wider school community. Discuss ways to integrate humor on a schoolwide basis. What messages will be given to parents, school board, and the community about the integration of humor? What can be done about those who disparage fun and humor in a learning environment?

☺ Implement a search for the comedians in your school. Begin by looking for the class clowns. Many comedians began laughing because of the personal difficulties in their lives. Class clowns are often laughing through the pain their lives. Discuss how to focus on the humor strength of the class clowns. Is there a Jim Carrey or Chris Rock in your school? Is this person treated with respect, even honored for her humor talents, or is there a mild disgust for the disruptions caused?

Café Conversations

Discussion questions: How can positive emotionality become embedded in your school culture? If the leadership in the school changes, what implications will this have for a focus on humergy? How can positive changes be sustained?

"Life begins as a quest of the child for the man and ends as a journey by the man to rediscover the child."

—Laurens van der Post

Chapter 7

SURVIVAL HUMOR
FOR STRESSED LEADERS

"Energizer Bunny arrested and charged with battery."

There are lots of energized leaders in education, bringing hope and joy to all they teach and reach. My favorite example comes from an administrator who attended a humor workshop in central Illinois. He was worried about his test scores, which were pretty abysmal. It was his job as a fairly new superintendent to relay this information to his school board. He dressed up in construction clothes with a tool belt around his waist and gave his best "Tim the 'Tool Man'" presentation. He pulled out the hammer and said "we're going to nail the next tests." The pliers were used to pull out the problems he had identified that were contributing to the problem. He claimed that they hardly noticed the terrible test scores, they were laughing so hard. The next school board meeting was to be another difficult subject so his planned PowerPoint presentation was actually his vacation pictures from Alaska. He had carefully identified the ones that would make the points that he wanted to make. He said his problem now is that the board always expects creative and fun meetings.

One of the most difficult tasks for a school leader is to implement positive change in the culture of a school or district. The school culture is complex and it has been the topic of countless articles and books. How does humor contribute to the school environment? This chapter will focus on two aspects of humor in relationship to the school culture. Trust has been identified as a crucial ingredient in an optimal school culture so I will explain the relationship between humor and trust. The other feature in this chapter is a visual framework that depicts how humergy can impact the culture on three levels. These are the context, process, and content of the learning process.

Educators usually choose education as a career because they want to make a difference in the lives of kids. Most want to laugh, have fun, and create an energized, engaged classroom. They want to work with others who desire a joy-flow collaborative school environment. The joy-flow experience identified in chapter 2 is the purposeful practice of optimism and positive emotionality. It's evident within cultures that strive for shared leadership, it's evident in school cultures continuously striving to maximize student learning, and it's evident within schools and cultures that are hopeful, engaged, and fun.

TRUST IS A MUST!

Trust is frequently mentioned as the most important ingredient in creating a collaborative culture. How do you know if your district has a high level of trust? Just look for a high capacity for humergy. Trust is the critical component necessary for supporting a collaborative culture of learning. *An indicator of a high level of trust is reflected by a high level of fun, laughter, play, and humor.* All stakeholders can work together to create a systemic culture of humergy and a positive learning environment. It is rare to find a school where humor is identified as a key ingredient that needs to be nurtured and practiced. Yet the energy, enthusiasm, and hope generated by humergy are a visible sign of trust. This sense of trust is dependent on the desire of fun-loving educators to collaborate and share their optimism, hope, and humergy practice for the purpose of maximizing learning. (See figure 7-1.)

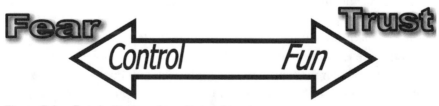

Figure 7-1. Fun: indicator of a culture of trust.

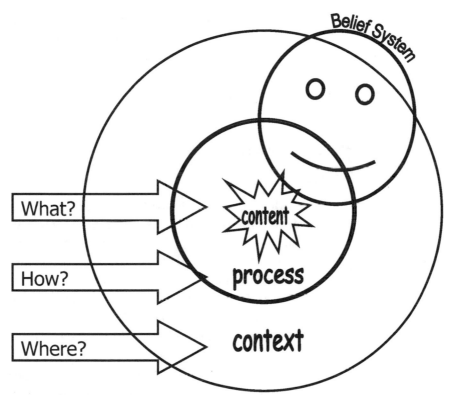

Figure 7-2. Framework for learning: humor indicators.

In order to fully explore the role of humergy in a school environment, let's look at a visual, a framework that depicts the emotional indicators that will maximize the joy-flow experience within a culture.

FRAMEWORK FOR LEARNING: INDICATORS OF HUMOR

This framework depicts the elements commonly identified as a foundation for the learning process, but arranges them into a visual portrayal of how humergy impacts the procedure. The context circle represents *where* learning occurs, asking the question: do the environment and available resources facilitate optimal learning? This circle encompasses the research on how positive emotionality influences the environment for learning, including the emotional state of both the teacher and the learner. As mentioned previously, anger and excess fear or stress can inhibit learning. In order to maximize learning through humergy, this circle represents what must be addressed first. In other words, addressing the context issues of a school culture is of utmost importance. Of course, numerous leadership articles and books provide resources on how to make this happen, but few address the importance of creating a happy or humergy state for optimal learning to occur.

> "And for further consideration: what if the hokey pokey is what it's all about?"

The middle circle depicts the process the individual teacher uses to facilitate learning. It also depicts the process the school leader employs to engage the staff in collaborative efforts to address cultural issues. It has a focus on *how* we learn, develop, plan, and implement policy. Imaging technology is providing us with biological information about the cognitive and social development of the student. Humor can be an integral component of the teaching process. An optimal method for the process circle will include the collaborative management of time, space, energy, and resources (Sylwester, 2005). It also is dependent on continual staff development for teachers so they have the resources and time for continuing professional development on cognitive neuroscience (including research on positive emotionality). The importance of movement, the arts, sleep, nutrition, and learning styles are all considerations for the teacher who is facilitating learning for each and every one of the unique brains floating around in his or her classroom. Each learner's brain is different and requires specific conditions for optimal learning. This type of research has been addressed and is the subject of numerous books and articles on differentiation and cognitive learning. Again the role of humor is sometimes mentioned as a part of the learning process, but it has not been specifically identified in many publications.

> "I press the control key but it's not giving me any."

The inner circle is what I think has garnered most of the attention in recent years. It answers the question: *What* needs to be learned? Is there a clear focus on the standards and the content that will be addressed? I strongly believe that learning standards are absolutely necessary and crucial for student learning. However, the current preoccupation with testing mandates and accountability have pushed the content issue to the forefront of education to the exclusion of context and process. Although the content is important, unless the context and process issues are seen as a preliminary focus, many students will not reach the content goals identified in the standards.

Learning about the subject matter of humor and positive emotionality is a component of the middle circle. The content resources on humor, joy, and fun continue to emerge as we learn more about cognitive research.

The smiley face that overlays all three circles represents the belief system of the educator. In the classroom, it's the teacher's beliefs about learning that will ultimately provide the direction for those students. Likewise, the beliefs of the administrator, central office, and school board will dictate the cultural environment of the district. Changing belief systems is difficult. Humor is the invisible elephant in the center of the room; everyone knows it's there, but no one pays any attention to it unless it disappears or steps on someone. We know when there is a humor void and we know if we're the brunt of sarcasm or negative humor. Belief systems must be addressed in order to release the potential of positive emotionality within a culture.

"We are born naked, wet, and hungry. Then things get worse."

CONTEXT

Let's take a look at humergy as a contextual component of teaching and learning. As mentioned previously, humor and laughter are integral to communication and building relationships. There are several examples from the world of business that highlight the importance of fun and laughter. Leslie Yerkes in her book *Fun Works* (2001) highlights companies who have profited from an infusion of fun in the workplace. The Pike Place Fish Market in Seattle has capitalized on this concept in a huge way. They have actually packaged their marketing program via their FISH video, website, and FISH camps for all who are interested. Their marketing programs are known worldwide for their emphasis on having fun as a means to profit (Yerkes). Productivity improves as fun and play are integrated into the workplace. Educators can adapt what has worked in the business community and take a serious look at the role that fun, play, and humor contribute to an optimal learning environment.

If the fish vendors can profit from having fun, why can't we benefit from having fun with our students? If we look at fun as anything that makes learning engaging, exciting, and challenging, it seems that the focus on rules and regulations are counterproductive. Unnecessary rules and regulations decrease or eliminate fun.

"Rules cause unintended consequences." —Joel Barker

"The more rules, the less fun."

Here is an example:

> A teacher was frequently observed leaving the building at 2:45 p.m. This was right at the end of the last period. It was reported to the school board and there was concern because the perception of the public might be that teachers were not working for a long enough time. So the school board created a rule to be sure all teachers stayed in the building until 4:00 p.m. They felt this would be an assurance that all teachers earned their money and were good teachers. What do you think happened? The entire staff lost any flexibility they once had. It caused teachers to lie (I feel sick) about a need to leave early to pick up a child, go to the doctor, or attend a parent-teacher conference for their own child. It caused anger among the staff and created a more stressful, unhappy culture in the district. (pers. comm.)

Angry teachers are stressed teachers. Angry teachers are not very effective in the classroom. Angry teachers are not going to contribute humergy to the culture of the school. Teachers who are committed professionals will find a way to be effective teachers in their own time frame. They do not need a rule telling them *when* they need to prepare for their teaching. They do need a nurturing school district that supports the challenges that educators face.

"I'm not tense, just terribly, terribly alert!"

Another district faced the same issue. They also wanted teachers who were committed to their profession. This district involved the teachers in the decision-making process. They asked the teachers to assist in planning ways to make the environment less stressful. After several brainstorming sessions it was determined that teachers could alternate times within the school grounds and could cover for each other. Several social events were initiated by the teachers. An ice cream social was held every other week at 4 p.m. Teachers were encouraged to bring their children to school with them for ice cream. Teachers took turns planning activities for their own children while freeing up time for the other teachers to do some prep work. It was a time to relax and celebrate the good things that happened during the week. At the end of the year, there was a family potluck. Teachers identified ways they could assist each other with planning time and helping to meet the child care needs of their colleagues. No one said that they *had* to go to the school potluck and *had* to have fun, but humor inspires collegiality and a desire to spend time together. Of course you know which district was filled with the energy of fun and humor.

Principals who use humor show higher teacher satisfaction scores, according to an article in *Educational Studies* (Hurren, 2006). Hurren says there is a fear that humor will be an unnecessary distraction; however, when principals dare to use humor, schools become better places to teach and learn.

Vita Meyer, who was principal of Bremen High School in Midlothian, Illinois, enjoys relating one of the ways she used humor to improve the culture of the school.

> When I worked as head swim coach and athletic director, I composed songs to send the athletes off to state competition. It was always a good laugh and great motivation for them to reach for the "gold" medal. When I became a high school principal, the football team had not won a conference championship in thirty years. At the opening parent athletic meeting I announced that I had been known as the singing coach and athletic director at my previous school and would be so proud to become the first singing principal in Illinois. This could occur if the team was playing for a

championship or had qualified for state competition. As luck would have it, the football team won the conference and made the state playoffs my first year! I not only sang to the football team, I was asked to sing on the video produced for the *All Area Players* by our local newspaper. My humorous challenge provided the momentum for a culture of fun in our school. I felt humor was a great motivating force and did a great deal towards the changing the culture of our school.

When laughter joins the stakeholders, there are fewer humordoomers. Laughter begets laughter and joy. Leaders can inspire a spirit of humergy.

I also know of one school that had several teachers who had babies during a school year. The administrator found the space and resources to provide in-school infant care for those teachers, many of whom were nursing mothers. This was just one example of his efforts to provide a joy-flow environment. Every one of his staff claimed they would never leave his building. Hope, fun, optimism, and trust were evident in this school culture.

This dedication to the contextual needs of the staff has been identified more frequently in education journals and books. There are journal articles and even conferences based on the emotional components of hope, trust, love, and spirituality. Stress is also emerging as a topic of concern.

Addressing the stress levels of educators is becoming more of a priority for school leaders. There is a growing need to find ways to counteract the increasing demands on both staff and students. This is evident in the numerous requests that I receive.

☺ "Can you come and give a humor workshop. I need to get my staff in a good mood before the beginning of the school year."

☺ "We are going to spend the day on school improvement; can you suggest something to improve the attitudes of the participants?"

☺ "Our funding has been cut again and morale is pretty low."

☺ "We have some serious issues here after our strike; I want our people to move on."

☺ "Where can I find information on the relationship between discipline and humor for my doctorial dissertation?"

☺ "Can you do something on humor to help improve our learning environment?"

☺ "Our stress levels have been increasing. Everyone is just so burnt out."

School leaders are striving to improve the culture and climate of their school. It is possible, in a workshop, to create an awareness of humor and to escalate the energy of a group on a short-term basis. However, in order to address multifaceted climate issues, the components of thoughtful planning, focused staff development, and reflective practice must be a part of a continuous process for improvement.

PROCESS

Throughout this book, there are various strategies for integrating the process that would embody the joy-flow concept. A review of chapter 6 provides numerous strategies for adapting the concept of humergy for individual teaching and learning needs. There is a section at the end of each chapter titled "Powerful Practice—Strategies for School Leaders." The "Jest for Fun" boxes highlight ideas that have been used by other educators.

The "Study Group Focus" and "Café Conversations" included at the end of each chapter are designed to assist educators as they collaborate on improving their knowledge and skills related to humor research.

Humor is the vehicle that can help us return to the safety net where learning is fun. Happiness, fun, play, mirth, comedy, joy, and jokes are all terms that have been used to define humor. Positive emotionality is a powerful mind/body connection that can create a remarkable feeling of control over one's life. This element of humergy can make a powerful difference in the culture of our schools. (Review table 3-1.)

"The really great (wo)man is the man who makes every (wo)man feel great."

—G.K. Chesterton

Fully developed characteristics are identified in school leaders in some recognizable ways, listed in the next section.

THE TOP TEN WAYS YOU CAN IDENTIFY A FUN SCHOOL LEADER

10. Has yo-yos, slinkies, and balloons in desk drawers. Consistently chooses a positive response pattern in life. The capacity to do this emerges from a focus on creating an affirmative environment (even a mental one) in which to operate.

9. Paints the boys' bathrooms in pink and the girls' in blue. He or she finds joy in change, incongruity, and uncertainty. Has the confidence to think outside of the box and see numerous possibilities. If a situation does not progress as planned, finds several other options.

8. Is found in the custodian closet laughing when school board members cut administrator salaries. Purposefully uses laughter to ease pain. He or she realizes that laughter is a way to relieve stress.

7. Plans frog races for staff meetings. He or she understands that humor is a coping skill that can be a response to change (from small annoyances to major crises).

6. Colors hair orange at Halloween and claims it was the original color. He or she uses self-deprecating humor as an exaggerated statement of truth, with the knack of laughing at mistakes and difficulties.

5. Puts the staff newsletter on the inside of faculty bathroom doors and titles the newsletter *The Flush*. Has the ability to understand and empathize with other people. Is able to assist others in seeing the humor in difficult situations and elicit laughter in the situation.

4. Brings a bag of jellybeans into teacher evaluation sessions. Listens to others and honors their feelings. Has the ability to recognize that anger in another person usually is the mirror of fear. He or she knows that good-natured teasing is a good way to build collegial relationships.

3. He or she tries every fun leadership activity that was ever invented and drives the staff crazy doing so. Has the ability to use humor in communicating with others. Highly skilled humergists

are able to ease the tension in group meetings by promoting laughter at the situation or at themselves.

2. Has staff meetings in the local pizza place and buys the pizza. He or she is able to use reframing as a shift in context that allows groups to look at a situation in a more useful way.

1. Offers a $1 bill to any teacher to whom he or she forgets to say, "Thank you for teaching here today. What can I do to make your job better?"

"If at first you don't succeed, skydiving isn't for you!"

SUMMARY

Trust is an indicator of a joyful school atmosphere. In order to address the issues that create a culture of trust, educators need to examine the context, process, and content of the school environment. The context includes the issue of "where," process addresses "how," and content includes the "what" of education. Our belief systems permeate all three of these areas, which are at the heart of teaching and learning. Excess stress impacts the ability of educators to be effective in the quality of teaching and learning. It negatively impacts the positive emotionality of the school environment. An abundance of unnecessary rules and mandates contributes to this stress.

Effective leaders promote collaborative learning and a positive emotional culture. They are eager to address the issues that contribute to negativity and stress. Building trust through the use of fun, laughter, and humor is embedded in their leadership style.

Powerful Practice—Strategies for School Leaders

☺ Recruit ideas from the staff for meeting energizers and ideas. Ask for volunteers to provide one of these at some of the meetings.

☺ Assist teachers by asking them how you can assist them in balancing work and family.

☺ Be on the lookout for stress relief and wellness strategies. Maybe provide an in-service day devoted to wellness and stress management. Have a yoga class, offer chair massages, and provide time for teachers to collaborate.

☺ Have a district wide in-service on contextual issues. Invite a leadership team from across the district to list key indicators of observable characteristics of a happy school. After providing basic training, invite teams to visit other schools to spend a half day observing the school culture. Ask them to be critical friends with practical suggestions for improving the environment. This requires a concerted effort by a committed leadership team with a strong belief in the power of creating a positive school culture.

Study Group Focus

☺ Observe the humergy in your school. Make a list of the observations. The worksheet for analysis of school culture can also be used (see table 7-2).

☺ Research humor articles on the Internet. As I have in previous chapters, I recommend the Association for Applied and Therapeutic Humor as a starting resource (www.aath.org). Share infor-

Table 7-2. Worksheet for Analysis of Culture

Fear and Stress Culture	Measure of Organizational Indicators of Humergy	Joy-Flow
Controlled, production-focused		Choice, discovery-focused
Content-based		Neuroscience-based
Bored participants		Engaged participants
Drudgery		Excitement
Low energy levels		Humergy (high energy and humor)
Linear		Chaotic
Low trust and fun		High trust, lots of fun
Victimization		Empowerment
Hopelessness		Hopefulness, optimism
Intense stress		Balance and focus
Disrespect: Few belief systems		Respect: Honoring all belief systems
Individual efforts		Collaboration and teamwork
High-stakes testing		Authentic assessment
Sarcasm and putdowns		Laughter and play

mation and discuss how to relay this information to the stakeholders in your community.

☺ Write your reflections on what you valued in this book. Do a
pair/share and then discuss with the group.

Café Conversations

☺ Discuss the characteristics of a happy school. What are the key indicators? How can humor be employed to build trusted relationships and a positive school culture?

☺ Share past experiences in situations that were stressful and how
these challenges were addressed. What techniques were successful? Why? How does stress impact your school environment?
What resources are currently available to educators to alleviate
stress? What resources are needed? Review the "Take It and Make
It—Funny" worksheet in appendix 13.

"Some cause happiness wherever they go; others, whenever they go."

—Oscar Wilde

Appendix I

HUMOR TERMINOLOGY

Coming to terms with humor!

adaptability. Describes how easily a child adjusts to changes and transitions. A sense of humor is closely related to our flexibility for change. The ability to laugh in new situations is apparent even with very young children. Some are at ease right away while others may hide behind a parent in a new situation.

approach/withdrawal. A child's initial response to novelty: "new places, people, situations or things" (Kristal, 2005). It takes a certain degree of risk-taking to experiment with humor. Class clowns, for instance, are pretty comfortable with new places and situations. They approach situations with enthusiasm, zest, and unbridled risk taking.

anger. A term for the emotional aspect of aggression, as a basic aspect of the stress response in animals, in which a perceived aggravating stimulus "provokes" a counter response, which is likewise aggravating and threatening of violence.

attachment theory. A theory, or group of theories, about the psychological tendency to seek closeness to another person, to feel secure when that person is present, and to feel anxious when that person is absent.

attention. The brain's focusing system activated by emotional arousal. Also the cognitive process of selectively concentrating on one thing while ignoring other things.

attitude. A key concept in psychology. Attitudes are positive or negative views of an "attitude object": i.e., a person, behavior, or event.

behavior. The actions or reactions of an object or organism, usually in relation to the environment. Behavior can be conscious or unconscious, overt or covert, and voluntary or involuntary.

brain. The control center of the central nervous system.

class clowns. Students who stimulate laughter in a classroom setting. Usually cheerful, positive individuals who relish being the center of fun.

cognitive science. Scientific study either of mind or of intelligence.

context circle. Describes where learning occurs.

content circle. Describes what needs to be learned.

cortisol. Stress hormone secreted by the adrenal glands during stress.

depression. A condition characterized by feelings of pessimism and sadness.

emotion. A neural impulse that moves an organism to action, prompting automatic reactive behavior that evolved as a survival mechanism.

emotion detector. A skill used to understand the emotions of self and others.

emotional intelligence. Also called *EI* or *EQ*, it describes an ability, capacity, or skill to perceive and assess.

emotional memory. Memories that are sparked by remembering the feelings about something that happened. Emotional arousal activates the attentional center of the brain and is a powerful trigger for learning and memory.

emotional knowledge. The level of perception and assessment that an individual has of their emotions at any given moment in time. To manage the emotions of one's self, of others, and of groups.

fear. An unpleasant feeling of perceived risk or danger, whether real or imagined.

flourish. The focus of positive psychology, including the concept of flow. A part of the positive emotions that includes peak humor experiences and humergy.

flow. The feeling of complete and energized focus in an activity, with a high level of enjoyment and fulfillment, as originally described by Mihaly Csikszentmihalyi.

frontal lobes. Part of the cerebral cortex of the brain that functions in initiating actions, solving problems, and making decisions.

fun. Anything that makes learning engaging, exciting, and challenging.

games. Usually performed by competing individuals or teams who have the same clearly defined goal. Although many animals play, only humans have games. The existence of rules and criteria that decide the outcome of games implies that games require intelligence of a significant degree of sophistication.

geliophobia. Fear of laughter.

gelotology. Physiology of laughter research.

group glee. Wave of laughter emerging from a group of young children.

happiness. Emotional or affective state in which we feel good or pleasure.

hippocampus. Structure in the brain involved with the formation and retrieval of memory.

hope. An emotional belief in a positive outcome related to events and circumstances within one's personal life.

humor. The quality that makes something amusing or laughable.

humergy. The energy that emerges from the humor, joy, and optimism of our inner spirit, reflects our unique personality, and nourishes a healthy mind/body balance.

humorobics. The physical act of laughing.

humor physiology. Events that occur in the human body in association with humorous experiences.

humor respiration. Laughing, giggling, or chortling that disrupts cyclic breathing, increases ventilation, and accelerates residual air exchange. This results in enhanced intake of oxygenated fresh air.

humor paradox. Discrepancy in a society that claims to place a high value on humor, but in reality, fears keep us from initiating and sustaining humor practice.

humor practice. The art and craft of purposefully applying humor to everyday life.

humordoomer. A person who consistently uses negative humor to control and manipulate others.

humorologist. Person who practices the art and science of healthy humor.

humorology. The art and science of humor.

humorphobia. A fear of fun, laughter, and humor.

hyperacademics. Overly intense focus on academics.

intensity. The reactive energy of a response, whether happy, sad, or angry, or expressive. The emotional response varies greatly among young children. For instance, some children will smile a little at peek-a-boo games while others laugh loudly.

impact vs. intent. Comparison between the purpose of the humor as perceived by the conveyor and the feelings evoked by the recipient of the humor.

joke. A short story or short series of words spoken or communicated with the intent of being laughed at or found humorous by the listener or reader.

joy. The emotion of great happiness.

joy-flow. Term used to describe positive emotionality as exhibited by enthusiasm, energy, joy, and hope. The peak experiences most of us identify with experiencing one's sense of humor.

laughter. The biological reaction of humans to moments or occasions of humor, an outward expression of amusement. Human response to a social connection (Provine 2000).

learning. The process of acquiring knowledge, skills, attitudes, or values, through study, experience, or teaching, that causes a change of behavior that is persistent, measurable, and specified or allows an individual to formulate a new mental construct or revise a prior mental construct (conceptual knowledge such as attitudes or values). It is a process that depends on experience and leads to long-term changes in behavior potential.

long-term memory. Memory that can last as little as thirty seconds or as long as decades.

love. Emotion of primary value associated with an intense attraction to a person, place, or thing.

memory. The ability of the brain to store, retain, and subsequently recall information.

mood. The basic quality of disposition. It may be more positive (a happy or cheerful child) or more negative (a cranky or serious child). Some researchers think that mood is parallel to or overlays our basic temperament.

optimism. The tendency to believe, expect, or hope that things will turn out well. The attitude of somebody who feels positive or confident.

peek-a-boo. Term used to describe the first stage of humor development in infants.

peak experience. Term used to describe an optimal experience of positive emotionality.

perception. The process of acquiring, interpreting, selecting, and organizing sensory information.

pessimism. Describes a belief that things are bad and will become worse.

play. Describes an unrestrained, amusing interaction with people, animals, or things, often in the context of learning.

positive emotionality. A state of being in which the individual is said to flourish. The research is based on the belief that positive emotions extend the capacity of attention, cognition, and action.

process circle. Describes how learning occurs.

pun-fun. Stage of humor development of children in grades 6–8.

psychoneuroimmunology. The study of the interactions between the brain and the immune system that combines psychology, neuroscience, and immunology.

riddle-de-dee. Stage of humor development of children in grades 3–5.

roast. An event in which an individual is subject to publicly hearing insults, praise, outlandish true and untrue stories, and heartwarming tributes. It is seen as a great honor to be roasted, as the individual is surrounded by friends, fans, and well-wishers, who can receive some of the same treatment as well during the course of the evening. The party and presentation itself are called a *roast*. The host of the event is called the *roast master*. In short, it is both the opposite and the same as a "toast."

sarcasm. Sneering, jesting, or mocking a person, situation, or thing. It is strongly associated with irony, with some definitions classifying it as a type of verbal irony.

safe humor. Practice of humor in safe situations.

self-deprecating humor. (Or self-effacing humor) The ability to laugh at ourselves; to make fun of our human foibles and maintain a sense of perspective. It is also powerful in defusing confrontations.

sense of humor. The capacity of a human being to respond to life challenges with optimistic enjoyment.

short-term memory. Sometimes referred to as "primary" or "active" memory—the part of memory that stores a limited amount of information for a limited amount of time (roughly fifteen to thirty seconds).

stages of humor development. Sequential process for the development of a sense of humor.

stress. Roughly the opposite of relaxation. A medical term for a wide range of strong external stimuli, both physiological and psychological, which can cause a physiological response called the general adaptation syndrome, first described in 1936 by Hans Selye in the journal *Nature*.

stressors. Any factor that causes stress is called a stressor. There are two kinds of stressors: processive stressors and systemic stressors. Processive stressors are elements in the environment perceived by the organism as potential dangers. These do not cause damage directly, but are processed in the cerebral cortex. The processed information is then sent via the limbic system in the hypothalamus, where they activate the supreme centers of the autonomic nervous system. This results in the fight-or-flight (or sympathetico-adrenal) response. Systemic stressors cause a disturbance in the organism's homeostasis, as well as tissue necrosis, hypotension and/or hypoxia. Often both types of stressors occur simultaneously. They are usually accompanied by pain and/or intense emotions.

stress management. Techniques intended to equip a person with effective coping mechanisms for dealing with psychological stress.

survivor humor (group). A specific type of humor response that is an active defense mechanism to help cope with threats and fears instead of surrendering to them (definition provided by Sandfa Ritz, nurse researcher).

teasing. The act of playfully disturbing another person, either with words or with actions. In mild cases, and especially when it is reciprocal, it is essentially a form of playing (friendly teasing). However, teasing can be also used as painful harassment (cruel teasing), if the teasing is one way. In extreme cases it may escalate to real violence, and may even result in abuse (in the case of a child, child abuse).

temperament. The general nature of an individual's personality, such as introversion or extroversion.

therapy. A treatment that is the attempted remediation of a health problem, usually following a diagnosis.

trust. Having confidence in and reliance on good qualities, especially fairness, truth, honor, or ability. The ability to take the responsibility for taking good care of somebody or something.

working memory. The collection of structures and processes used for temporarily storing and manipulating information.

Appendix 2

COMEDIAN LIST

Abbott & Costello
Tim Allen
Woody Allen
Jeff Altman
Lucille Ball
Mel Brooks
Carol Burnett
Drew Carey
George Carlin
Jim Carrey
Bill Cosby
Rodney Dangerfield
Ellen Degeneres
W. C. Fields
Jeff Foxworthy
Bob Hope
Andy Kaufman
Buster Keaton
Alan King

Loretta LaRouche
Laurel & Hardy
Jay Leno
David Letterman
Jerry Lewis
Steve Martin
Eddie Murphy
Rosie O'Donnell
Paula Poundstone
Don Rickles
Joan Rivers
Adam Sandler
Jerry Seinfeld
Sinbad
Smothers Brothers
The Three Stooges
Carrot Top
Dick Van Dyke
Robin Williams

Appendix 3

PLAYFUL SUGGESTIONS

☺ Have a play corner equipped with toys and games (yes, *especially* at the middle school and high school levels). There is a suggested toy list in appendix 10.

☺ Have students take turns doing riddles with their classmates. Post the most difficult riddle on the bulletin board in the hallway. Invite a cooperating class to share riddles with your class. This could evolve into a schoolwide riddle contest.

☺ Create a "Comedy Central" writing corner where students "play" with words, stories, and poetry and humor.

☺ Have a "dress as your favorite comedian" day. Students come equipped to tell one of the jokes of that comedian.

☺ Let the students plan activities they think would be fun ways to learn the upcoming lessons. Encourage creativity and innovative ideas.

☺ Have toys on your desk. Encourage students who need to have activity to use these whenever they would like. The rule would be that they could not disturb the learning of others. Include stress balls and Rubik's Cubes (consult toy list in appendix 10).

☺ Have a chart in the corner of the room where students can list the types of *play* they enjoy. Encourage everyone to try a new way of playing each week. (See appendix 3 for playful ideas.)

☺ Use improvisational comedy as a way to study material.

Appendix 4

SENSE OF HUMOR REFLECTIONS

Analysis of past emotional experiences:

- ☺ What are my strongest emotional memories?
- ☺ What do I fear?
- ☺ What makes me laugh?

Awareness of current emotional state or feelings:

- ☺ What is my current comfort zone in expressing my emotions?
- ☺ What *self-talk* do I engage in during the day?
- ☺ How can my ongoing awareness of my feelings assist with creating an environment for optimal learning?

Ability to let go of what cannot be controlled. Look for the absurdity of human behavior beginning with yourself. Risk-taking confidence comes from an assurance of purpose that is constant amid the change and chaos of humor practice:

- ☺ What fears inhibit my learning?

☺ Do I blame others (the students, the parents, the teachers, the administrators, the school board) for the inability to control many factors of my teaching and learning environment?

☺ Do I accept the decisions of others even though I might not agree? Can I trust others to make the right decisions?

Skill of reading the emotions of others (emotional literacy):

☺ Do I really listen to what the other person is saying?

☺ Can I read body language that mirrors the emotions of others?

☺ Do I notice when I tweak their sense of humor?

☺ How can I make a conscious effort to elicit humergy in others?

Focus on hope and optimism to maintain the joy of humergy:

☺ Am I willing to take the time for humor? Do I frequently choose play and fun?

☺ What new form of play am I willing to try?

☺ Am I willing to take the risks necessary to experiment with humor?

☺ What does a peak experience feel like for me?

Appendix 5

HUMOR STYLES INVENTORY

Self awareness is a critical component in the journey of discovering your humor strength. This instrument is designed as an awareness of your own experience with a sense of humor. If you are serious about humor, you may want to begin to journal data on what tickles your funny bone. Jot down what makes you smile and when you laugh out loud. Review the categories in the humor list and the humor terminology list to assist you in identifying the type of humor that appeals to you. Colleagues can generate observations and suggestions for your humor practice.

1. What makes you laugh? _____
   _____

2. Identify your favorite: _____ _____
   Comedians _____
   Movies _____
   Television shows _____

3. What form of humor do you practice? (Refer to the appendix 6 categories and appendix 8 terminology lists.)
   _____
   _____

4. When are you comfortable using humor? _____

_____

5. How do you play? _____

_____

6. What is your first choice when you want to have fun? _____

_____

7. The ability to laugh at yourself is called "self-deprecating humor." (Examples are physical characteristics, the aging process, mistakes made, etc.) When do you use this kind of humor?

_____

_____

8. Reflect on the type of humor your parents exposed you to. What kind of humor did you experience when you were growing up? _____

_____

9. What kind of humor being do you want to become? _____

_____

Appendix 6

SEVERAL CATEGORIES OF HUMOR

exaggeration. Using an obvious over- or under-statement, including such things as physical characteristics, data, feelings, experiences, etc.

incongruity. Connecting two generally accepted opposites, the lack of a rational relation of objects, people, or ideas to each other or to the environment.

surprise. Exploiting the occurrence of the unexpected—whether fact, thought, feeling, or event; in its more sophisticated form it becomes *irony*.

slapstick. The form of humor that depends for its effect on fast, boisterous, and zany physical activity and horseplay, often accompanied by broad, obvious, rowdy verbal humor.

the absurd. That which obviously lacks reason, which is foolish or ridiculous in its lack of good sense, includes *nonsense*, the nonsensical use of logic and language; the *preposterous*, arising from the incongruity of reality and fantasy; and *whimsy*, a fanciful or fantastic device, object, or creation especially in writing, art, or decoration.

human predicaments. Featuring situations in which a character appears foolish or bested, includes the humor of *superiority* and *degradation*, which is based on self-aggrandizement or the release of hostility through the discomfiture, failure, or misfortune of others, and *comic predicaments*, which is based on an attitude of sympathetic acceptance of the human predicament and can be seen in situations in which either oneself or someone else appears foolish or bested by life for the moment; in this case, however, no hostile feelings are intended to be aroused or expressed.

ridicule. Primarily the teasing and mockery of others or oneself, can be seen expressed, for example, in the mockery of adults, their world, and its customs and institutions, etc. *Negative ridicule* finds its source in feelings of self-aggrandizement or the release of hostility through the mockery of others. *Playful ridicule*, on the other hand, is based on the sympathetic acceptance of human foibles. *Satire* is primarily a sophisticated artistic form of humor arising from both types of ridicule.

defiance. Primarily the release of hostility or aggression through rebellion, includes the violation of conventions, the perpetration of situations socially unacceptable to adults, the expression of forbidden ideas, and the violation of adult authority.

verbal humor. The manipulation of language through word play, puns, jokes, sarcasm, wit, name-calling, and the like; may contain either a positive or negative emotional content, but differs from the other forms in being a verbal rather than a situational form of humor.

Adapted from Katharine H. Kappas. 1967. A developmental analysis of children's responses to humor. *Library Quarterly* 37 (Jan.): 68–69.

Appendix 7

HUMOR BELIEF INVENTORY

Please answer by selecting the most appropriate score: 1 = seldom/never or disagree and 5 = often/all of the time or agree.

Assessment	1	2	3	4	5
1. Humor is a skill that I use with intent and purpose.					
2. I have a good sense of humor.					
3. I intentionally use humor to optimize learning.					
4. I intentionally use humor to build a relationship with students, educators, and parents.					
5. I know and understand my humor style.					
6. I believe humor is inherited.					
7. If a classroom of students is laughing and joking, an observer will assume the class is not learning.					

8. Humor can be an effective tool for students with serious behavior challenges.					
9. Humor relieves stress.					
10. Humor promotes healing.					
11. Humor increases productivity.					
12. Humor requires a culture of trust.					
13. The ability to laugh at yourself can be used to gain the trust of others.					
14. The "class clown" is usually perceived in our work environment as being a disruption to learning.					
15. Humor is the #1 characteristic students desire in a teacher.					
16. Playing and having fun in the classroom is a waste of precious learning time.					
17. Humor is not a measurable characteristic and therefore has a questionable role in education.					
18. If there is a perception that I am a fun seeker, I will not be considered professional.					
19. While humor is important, learning requires a serious work environment with little time for fun, humor, and play.					
20. I am not comfortable initiating fun, play, and humor in my current work culture.					

Appendix 8

HUMOR TERMINOLOGY LIST

amusing
antic
bawdy
bizarre
buffoon
bumpkin
burlesque
caricature
cartoons
cheerful
child-like
cynical
caring
darling
deadpan
derisive
devilish
droll
dry
elfish

expansive
facetious
farcical
far-out
flaky
gleeful
gross
grotesque
hostile
hysterical
impish
insulting
irony
jocular
jolly
jovial
kibitzing
licentious
lively
ludicrous

merry
mischievous
nitwit
nonsensical
observational
off-beat
outrageous
parody
perverse
playful
poor-soul
punny
quirly
raucous
ribald
risqué
sarcasm
sarcastic
sardonic
satire

satirical

self-deprecating

sick

silly

simple

situation comedy

slapstick

smart-aleck

superior

teasing

topical

uninhibited

unique

vaudeville

vexatious

visual

wack

waggish

weird

whimsical

witty

wry

x-rated

yummy

zany

Appendix 9

FAMILIAR SONG LIST

theme song to the *Mickey Mouse Show*
"Twinkle, Twinkle, Little Star"
"Oh Where, Oh Where Has My Little Dog Gone?"
"Jack and Jill"
"Mary Had a Little Lamb"
"Skip to My Lou"
"Pop Goes the Weasel"
"Yankee Doodle"
"Oh! Susanna"
"Home on the Range"

"Dixie"
"Polly Wolly Doodle"
"Oh My Darling Clementine"
"This Land Is Your Land"
"I've Been Working on the Railroad"
"Proud Mary"
"Rock Island Line"
"Billy Boy"
"Looby Loo"
"Twist and Shout"
"YMCA"

Appendix 10

TOY LIST

I have had great luck finding toys and games at garage sales. Some games can be made or created by the students. This is just a brief list to get you started. The possibilities are endless.

balloons*	paddle balls	Rubik's cube
bean bags	pick-up sticks	slide puzzles
bubbles	puppets	Slinkies
clapping hands*	makeup and dress-up	squish balls
hula hoops	mood rings	spinning tops
jacks	Mr. Potato Head	tic tac toe
kazoos*	play money	

* suggested for group use

Appendix 11

SILLY WORD LIST

Use the following words to stimulate creative writing:

clowning	sparky	soreemebe
goofy	cartoon	boogersnotzle
sassafras	snickers	doopsie
giant	comedian	bugslug
survivor	gibbery	jugahuga
Bugs Bunny	smolly	kittenizen
joking	hogstown	
fiddle de de	singseeso	

Appendix 12

BUMPER STICKER BOMBARDMENT

We have used bumper stickers to promote children who are already doing well, and to inflate the egos of their parents (who would not put anything else on their car) but will put up the sticker that says:

I have an honor roll student at Prestige High.

We also have a strong negative reaction to this promotional bumper sticker:

My kid can beat up your honor roll student!

Bumper stickers can be successful, and a relatively cheap way to use humor as a vehicle (no pun intended) for getting our message to millions of Americans. What if we spent time at a staff meeting or a board meeting using humor to create bumper stickers for a referendum? It would do several things.

- ☺ The meetings would be more fun.
- ☺ The benefits of humergy would be evident.
- ☺ It would provide attention-grabbing messages for the public that would get the message across.

Here is a brief list of bumper stickers—be sure to collect your own!

There are three kinds of people: Those who can count and those who
can't.

Five days a week, my body is a temple. The other two, it's an amusement park.

A day without sunshine is like night.

Always remember you are unique, just like everyone else.

Coffee, chocolate, men; some things are just better rich.

Don't treat me any differently than you would the queen.

Earth first! We'll strip-mine the other planets later.

Ever stop to think and forget to start again?

Get a new car for your spouse. It'll be a great trade.

God made us sisters; Prozac made us friends.

God must love stupid people . . . he made so many.

Hard work has a future payoff. Laziness pays off now.

I fought the lawn and the lawn won.

I need someone real bad . . . Are you real bad?

I took an IQ test and the results were negative.

I want to die peacefully in my sleep like my grandfather . . . not
screaming and yelling like the passengers in his car.

If at first you don't succeed, skydiving isn't for you.

If we are what we eat, I'm cheap, fast, and easy.

If you can read this, I can hit my brakes and sue you.

If you drink, don't park. Accidents cause people.

If you want breakfast in bed, sleep in the kitchen.

It's lonely at the top, but you eat better.

Keep honking while I reload.

Liberal arts major. Will think for food.

Lottery: a tax on people who are bad at math.

Love may be blind, but marriage is a real eye opener.

Madness takes its toll. Please have exact change.

My mother is a travel agent for guilt trips.

Old age comes at a bad time.

Out of my mind. Back in five minutes!

Sometimes I wake up grumpy, other times I let her sleep.

Veni, vedi, visa: I came, I saw, I did a little shopping.
Warning: dates in calendar are closer than they appear!
We are born naked, wet, and hungry. Then things get worse.
Where there's a will, I want to be in it.
Your kid may be an honor student, but you're still an idiot.
You're just jealous because the voices only talk to me.

Appendix 13

TAKE IT AND MAKE IT—FUNNY

This activity is designed to purposefully take the difficulties in your life and look at these challenges in a humorous way. Think of a problem or issue facing you right now and play with ways to turn it into fun. Here are some ideas to get you started:

☺ Take two incongruent items and see how you can make them relate. Here are some examples:

Complying with No Child Left Behind is like a microwave because . . .
Our staff is like the Beatles because . . .
Our budget is like blueberries because . . .

☺ Create a top ten list of why this particular challenge is a good thing. For example, a group had just had major budget cuts and there were no more light bulbs to be purchased for the year. They had a top ten list of why it was great to be in the dark, including:

Can't see the dust bunnies
Can't observe any fights or behavior problems
Don't need sun glasses

☺ Do a *Survivor* show. Make a list of all of the worst things that have ever happened to staff members. Staff writes these on papers (anonymously) and a list is compiled. Teams are created to brainstorm survivor strategies.

☺ Exaggerate the problem. Be creative.

☺ Brainstorm how cheese can be used as a strategy to market your test scores. Have a wine and cheese party, and bring the book *Who Moved My Cheese?* (Johnson, 1998). Wear a cheese head (Wisconsin Packer fans will assist you here). Ideas generate lots of additional ideas and *fun happens*!

REFERENCES

BOOKS AND ARTICLES

Armstrong, T. (2006). *The best schools: How human development research should inform educational practice*. Alexandria, VA: Association for Supervision and Curriculum Development.

Bacall, A. (2002). *The lighter side of educational leadership*. Thousand Oaks, CA: Corwin.

Bany-Winters, L. (2002). *Funny bones*. Chicago: Chicago Review Press.

Baum, R. B. (2002). Infusing humor in the education of students with emotional and behavioral disorders. *Perceptions*, 35(2), 2–6.

Bennett, E. L., Diamond, M. C., Krech, D., & Rosenzweig, M. R. (1964). Chemical and anatomical plasticity of brain. *Science, 146*, 610–19.

Berk, L. S., et al. (1989). Neuroendocrine and stress hormone changes during mirthful laughter. *The American Journal of the Medical Sciences, 298*, 390–96.

Berk, R. A. (1996). Student ratings of 10 strategies for using humor in college teaching. *Journal on Excellence in College Teaching*, 7(3), 71–92.

Berk, R. A. (2000). Does humor in course tests reduce anxiety and improve performance? *College Teaching, 48*, 151–58.

Berk, R. A. (2001). The active ingredients in humor: Psycho physiological benefits/risks for older adults. *Educational Gerontology, 27*, 323–39.

Berk, R. A. (2004). Coping with the daily stressors of an academic career: Try mirthium®. *Academic Physician and Scientist* July/August, 2–3.

Bernstein, A. J. (2001). *Emotional vampires: Dealing with people who drain you dry*. New York: McGraw-Hill.

Bryk, A. S., & Schneider, B. L. (2002). *Trust in schools: A core resource for improvement*. New York: Russell Sage Foundation.

Burgess, R. (2000). *Laughing lessons: 149 2/3 ways to make teaching and learning fun*. Minneapolis, MN: Free Spirit.

Caine, G., & Caine, R. (1997). *Education on the edge of possibility*. Alexandria, VA: Association for Supervision and Curriculum Development.

Charnetski, C. J., & Brennan, F. X. (2001). *Feeling good is good for you: How pleasure can boost your immune system and lengthen your life*. Emmaus, PA: Rodale.

Connors, N. A. (2000). *If you don't feed the teachers they eat the students!* Nashville, TN: Incentive Publications.

Cousins, N. (1979). *Anatomy of an illness*. New York: W. W. Norton.

Cousins, N. (1990). *Head first: The biology of hope and the healing power of the human spirit*. New York: Penguin.

Csikszentmihalyi, M. (1990). *Flow: The psychology of optimal experience*. New York: Harper & Row.

Csikszentmihalyi, M. (1997). *Finding flow: The psychology of engagement with everyday life*. New York: Basic Books.

Damasio, A. (1999). *The feeling of what happens: Body and emotion in the making of consciousness*. San Diego, CA: Harcourt.

Davidson, R. (Ed.). (2000). *Anxiety, depression and emotion*. Oxford, UK: Oxford University Press.

Davidson, R. J., Scherer, K., & Goldsmith, H. H. (Eds.). (2003). *Handbook of affective sciences*. Oxford, UK: Oxford University Press.

Derks, P. (1997). Laughter and electorencephalagraphic activity. *Humor, 10*, 285–300.

Diamond, M., & Hopson, J. (1998). *Magic trees of the mind: How to nurture your child's intelligence, creativity, and healthy emotions from birth through adolescence*. New York: Penguin Putnam.

Dugatkin, L. A. (2002). Turtles with toys: It's more than just (animal) play. *Cerebrum 4*(3), 41–52.

Duman, R. S., Malberg, J., & Thome, J. (1999). Neural plasticity to stress and antidepressant treatment. *Biological Psychiatry, 46*(9), 1181–91.

Dunn, J. R. (1999). What is a sense of humor? An interview with James A. Thorson. *Humor & Health Journal, 8*(2).

Endres, S. (2005). *Teaching is too important to be taken seriously.* Chicago: Spectrum Press.

Estroff Marano, H. (1999). Depression: Beyond serotonin. *Psychology Today Magazine*, March/April 1999.

Farah, M. J., Noble, K. G., & Hurt, H. (2005). Poverty, privilege and brain development: Empirical findings and ethical implications. In J. Illes (Ed.), *Neuroethics in the 21st century.* New York: Oxford University Press.

Farris, P. J., Fuhler, C. J., & Walther, M. P. (1999). That's a good one! Humor in the primary classroom. *Delta Kappa Gamma Bulletin*, 65(3), 5–8.

Forsyth, A. G., Altermatt, E. R., & Forsyth, P. D. (1997). Humor, emotional empathy, creativity and cognitive dissonance. Paper presented at the annual meeting of the American Psychological Association, August 16.

Franzini, L. R. (2002). *Kids who laugh: How to develop your child's sense of humor.* New York: Garden City Publishers.

Fredrickson, B. (2003). The value of positive emotions. *American Scientist*, 91, 330–35.

Fry, W. F. (1992). The physiologic effects of humor, mirth, and laughter. *Journal of the American Medical Association*, 267(13), 1857–58.

Fry, W. F. (1994). The biology of humor. *HUMOR: International Journal of Humor Research*, 7(2), 111–26.

Fry, W. F., & Salameh, W. A. (Eds). (1993). *Advances in humor and psychotherapy.* Sarasota, FL: Professional Resource Press.

Garland, R. (1991). *Making work fun.* San Diego, CA: Shamrock Press.

Glatthorn, A. A. (2002). *Publish or perish: The educator's imperative.* Thousand Oaks, CA: Corwin.

Goleman, D. (1995). *Emotional intelligence: Why it can matter more than I.Q.?* New York: Bantam.

Goleman, D. (1998). *Working with emotional intelligence.* New York: Bantam.

Goleman, D., Boyatzis, R., & McKee, A. (2002). *Primal leadership: Realizing the power of emotional intelligence.* Boston: Harvard Business School.

Goodman, J. (1988a). Anatomy of Norman Cousins. *Laughing Matters*, 2(3).

Goodman, J. (1988b). The Family Circus. *Laughing Matters*, 3(4).

Goor, M. (1989). Humor in the Classroom: Options for Enhancing Learning. Paper presented at the National Conference of the Council for Exceptional Children/Council for Children with Behavior Disorders, September, Charlotte, NC.

Green, L. (1994). *Making sense of humor: How to add joy to your life.* Manchester, CN: KIT.

Hansen, P. G. (1985). *The joy of stress.* New York: Andrews and McMeel.

Harvey, L. C. (1998). *Humor for healing: A therapeutic approach*. San Antonio, TX: Therapy Skill Builders.

Hubel, D. H., & Wiesel, T. N. (1962). Receptive fields, binocular interaction and functional architecture in the cat's visual cortex. *Journal of Physiology, 160*, 106–54.

Hurren, L. (2006). The effects of principals' humor on teachers' job satisfaction.*Educational Studies, 32*(4), 373–85.

Jasheway, L. A. (1996). *Don't get mad, get funny!* Duluth, MN: Pfeifer-Hamilton.

Jensen, E. (1994). *Brain-based learning*. Del Mar, CA: Turning Point.

Jensen, E. (1994). *The learning brain*. Del Mar, CA: Turning Point.

Jensen, E. (1998). *Teaching with the brain in mind*. Del Mar, CA: Turning Point.

Johnson, S. (1998). *Who moved my cheese? An amazing way to deal with change in your work and in your life*. New York: Putnam.

Jones, S. (2003). *Blueprint for student success*. Thousand Oaks, CA: Corwin Press.

Kappas, K. H. (1967). A developmental analysis of children's responses to humor. *Library Quarterly, 37*, 68–69.

Kessler, R. (2000). *The soul of education: Helping students find connection, compassion, and character at school*. Alexandria, VA: Association for Supervision and Curriculum Development.

Kilcup, K. (2001). Studies in American humor. *The Journal of the American Humor Studies Association, 3*(8).

Klein, A. (1989). *The healing power of humor*. New York: Tarcher/Putnam.

Klein, A. (1998). *The courage to laugh*. New York: Tarcher/Putnam.

Kolberg, K. J., & Loomans, D. (1993). *The laughing classroom: Everyone's guide to teaching with humor and play*. Tiburon, CA: H. J. Kramer.

Kotulak, R. (1996). *Inside the brain: Revolutionary discoveries of how the mind works*. Kansas City, KS: Andrews and McMeely.

Kristal, J. (2005). *The temperament perspective: Working with children's behavioral styles*. New York: Paul H. Brookes Publishing.

LeDoux, J. (1996). *The emotional brain: The mysterious underpinnings of emotional life*. New York: Simon and Schuster.

LeDoux, J. (2002). *Synaptic self: How our brains become who we are*. New York: Viking.

Linksman, R. (2007). Setting up an effective pre-school reading program. *Illinois ASCD Newsletter, 52*(4).

Mallan, K. (1993). *Laugh lines: Exploring humor in children's literature*. Newtown, New South Wales, Australia: Primary English Teaching Association.

Martin, R. A. (1996). The Situational Humor Response Questionnaire (SHRQ) and Coping Humor Scale (CHS): A decade of research findings. *Humor: International Journal of Humor Research*, 9(3–4), 251–72.

Martin, R. A. (2000). Is laughter the best medicine? Humor, laughter, and physical health. *Current Directions in Psychological Science 11*, 216–220.

Martin R. A. (2001). Humor, laughter, and physical health: Methodological issues and research findings. *Psychological Bulletin 127*: 504–19.

Martin, R. A. (2007). *The psychology of humor: An integrative approach*. Amsterdam: Elsevier.

Maslow, A. (1968). *Toward a psychology of being*, 2nd ed. New York: D. Van Nostrand Co.

McElherne, L. N. (1999). *Jump starters: quick classroom activities that develop self-esteem, creativity, and cooperation*. Minneapolis, MN: Free Spirit.

McGhee, P. E. (1999). *Health, healing and the amuse system*. Dubuque, IA: Kendall/Hunt.

McGhee, P. E. (2002a). *Stumble bees and pelephones: How to develop a powerful verbal sense of humor*. Dubuque, IA: Kendall/Hunt.

McGhee, P. E. (2002b). *Understanding and promoting the development of children's humor: A guide for parents*. Dubuque, IA: Kendall/Hunt.

Mendler, A. N. (2001). *Connecting with students*. Alexandria, VA: Association for Supervision and Curriculum Development.

Millard, E. N. (1999). Humor can be a serious strategy. *The Delta Kappa Gamma Bulletin*, 65(3), 9–14.

Morreall, J. (1997). *Humor works*. Amherst, MA: HRD Press.

Morrison, M. K. (2000). Humor is a funny thing. Madeira Beach, FL: Florida Association for Supervision and Curriculum Development.

Morrison, M. K. 2005. Humor is a funny thing. Retrieved from www.susan-jjones.com/growbrain2.html.

Mroczek, D. K., & Spiro, A., III. (2005). Change in life satisfaction over 20 during adulthood: Findings from the VA Normative Aging Study. *Journal of Personality and Social Psychology*, 88, 189–202.

Nilsen, A. P., & Nilsen, D. L. F. (2000). *Encyclopedia of 20th century American humor*. Phoenix, AZ: Oryx.

Nunley, K. F. (2001). *Layered curriculum: The practical solution for teachers with more than one student in their classroom*. Kearney, NE: Morris Publishing.

Olliff, V. J. (1999). Lighten up! *The Delta Kappa Gamma Bulletin*, 65(3). Special issue: Impact of humor on education and learning.

Panksepp, J. (2003). Review of Emotions and the brain by Steve Johnson. *Discover*, 24(4).

Paulson, T. L. (1989). *Making humor work*. Mississauga, Ontario, Canada: Crisp Learning.

Pert, C. (1997). *Molecules of emotion: Why you feel the way you feel*. New York: Scribner.

Posner, M I., & Rothbart, M. K. (2007). *Educating the human brain*. Washington, DC: American Psychological Association.

Prerost, F. J. (1993). A strategy to enhance humor production among elderly persons: Assisting in the management of stress. *Activities, Adaptation and Aging, 17*(4), 17–24.

Provine, R. R. (2000). *Laughter, a scientific investigation*. New York: Viking Penguin.

Purkey, W. W. (2006). *Teaching class clowns (and what they can teach us)*. Thousand Oaks, CA: Corwin.

Ranpura, A. (1997). Weightlifting for the mind: Enriched environments and cortical plasticity. Retrieved from www.brainconnection.com/topics/printindex.php3?main=fa/cortical-plasticity.

Rayl, A. J. S. (2002). Humor: A mind-body connection. *The Scientist, 14*(19), 1.

Roe, B., Alfred, S., & Smith, S. (1998). *Teaching through stories: Yours, mine and theirs*. Norwood, MA: Christopher-Gordon.

Rowe, M. R. (2001). *Puntoons! Jest for the health of it!* Bloomington, IN: Authorhouse.

Salameh, W. A., & Fry, W. F., Jr. (2001). *Humor and wellness in clinical intervention*. Westport, CT: Praeger.

Sapolsky, R. J. (1998). *Why zebras don't get ulcers: An updated guide to stress, stress-related diseases, and coping*. New York: W. H. Freeman.

Sapolsky, R. J. (1999). Stress and your shrinking brain. *Discover*, March, 116–22.

Schwartz, E A. (1999). Humor development in children from infancy to eighth grade. *Research for Nursing Practice, 1*(2), 1–6.

Seligman, M., & Csikszentmihalyi, M. (2000). Positive psychology: An introduction. *American Psychologist, 55*(1), 5–14.

Shade, R. A. (1996). *License to laugh: Humor in the classroom*. Englewood, CO: Teachers Ideas.

Shammi, P. (1999). Humour appreciation: a role of the right frontal lobe. *Brain, 122*(4), 657–66.

Shammi, P., & Stuss, D. T. (2003). The effects of normal aging on humor appreciation. *Journal of the International Neuropsychological Society, 9*, 855–63.

Siegel, D. J. (1999). *The developing mind: Toward a neurobiology of interpersonal experience*. New York: Guilford.

Sousa, D. A. (2001). *How the brain learns*. Thousand Oaks, CA: Corwin.

Sprenger, M. (1999). *Learning and memory: The brain in action*. Alexandria, VA: Association for Supervision and Curriculum Development.

Sprenger, M. (2002). *Becoming a wiz at brain-based teaching: How to make every year your best year*. Thousand Oaks, CA: Corwin.

Stephenson, S., & Thibault, P. (2006). *Laughing matters: Strategies for building a joyful learning community*. Bloomington, IN: Solution Tree.

Sternberg, E. M. (2000). *The balance within: The science connecting health and emotions*. New York: W. H. Freeman.

Stewart, D. W., & Furse, D. H. (1986). *Effective television advertising: A study of 1000 commercials*. Lexington, MA: Lexington Books.

Stopsky, F. (1992). *Humor in the classroom: A new approach to critical thinking*. Lowell, MA: Discovery Enterprises.

Stronge, J. H. (2004). *Qualities of effective teachers*. Alexandria, VA: Association for Supervision and Curriculum Development.

Sultanoff, S. M. (1994). Therapeutic uses of humor. *The California Psychologist, 25*.

Sultanoff, S. M. (2002). Integrating humor into psychotherapy. In C. Schaefer (Ed.), *Play Therapy with Adults*. New York: Wiley and Sons.

Sylwester, R. (1995). *A celebration of neurons, an educator's guide to the human brain*. Alexandria, VA: Association for Supervision and Curriculum Development.

Sylwester, R. (2003). *A biological brain in a cultural classroom*. Thousand Oaks, CA: Corwin.

Sylwester, R. (2005). *How to explain a brain*. Thousand Oaks, CA: Corwin.

Sylwester, R. (2006). Mirror neuron update. Retrieved from www.brainconnection.com/content/226_1.

Teicher, S. (2005). Practice Scenes for the Tough Choices of Adolescence. *Christian Science Monitor*, July 12.

Volkmar, F. R., & Greenough, W. T. (1972). Rearing complexity affects branching of dendrites in the visual cortex of the rat. *Science, 176*, 1445–47.

Weber, M. (2003). Coping with malcontents: You can deal with negative staff and prevent yourself from becoming negative. *School Administrator, 60*(2), 6–11.

Weinstein, M. (1997). *Managing to have fun*. New York: Simon and Schuster.

Wheatley, M J. (2002). *Turning to one another: Simple conversations to restore hope to the future*. San Francisco: Berrett-Koehler.

Wolfe, P. (2001). *Brain matters: Translating research into classroom practice*. Alexandria, VA: Association for Supervision and Curriculum Development.

Wolk, S. (2001). The benefits of exploratory time. *Journal of Educational Leadership, 59*(2), 56–59.

Wood, C. (1997). *Yardsticks: Children in the classroom ages 4–14*. Turner Falls, MA: Northeast Foundation for Children.

Wooten, P. (1996). *Compassionate laughter: Jest for your health*. Salt Lake City, UT: Commune-a-key.

Wright, W. E. (2002). The effects of high stakes testing in an inner-city elementary school: The curriculum, the teachers, and the English language learners. *Current Issues in Education*, 5(5).

Wurtman, J. (1998). *Neurotransmitters and food: Managing your mind and mood through food*. New York: Harper and Row.

Yerkes, L. (2001). *Fun works: Creating places where people love to work*. San Francisco: Berrett-Koehler.

Ziv, A. (1984). *Personality and a sense of humor*. New York: Springer.

Ziv, A., & Ziv, N. (2002). *Humor and creativity in education*. Paris: Creatrix Editions.

FUN WEBSITES

Alliance for Childhood: www.allianceforchildhood.net/projects/play/play_fact_sheet.htm

American Medical Association journals: www.ama-assn.org/med_link/peer.htm

Association for Applied and Therapeutic Humor: www.aath.org/

Association for the Study of Play: www.csuchico.edu/kine/tasp/index.html

Brain Lab: www.newhorizons.org/blab.html

Brain Net: www.brainnet.org/

Comedy Cures: www.comedycures.org/saranne.html

The Dana Foundation, *Brain Work, the Neuroscience Newsletter*: www.dana.org

Deb Gaudlin: www.debgauldin.com/

Fun Squad with Charles Lutz: www.funsquadinc.com/

Humor for Teachers: www.learninglaffs.com/

Humor for Your Health: www.humorforyourhealth.com/humor_articles.html

Humor Project: www.humorproject.com/

Humor Quest, Mary Kay's website: www.questforhumor.com/index.html

Humor X with Karyn Buxman: www.humorx.com/KB_humorx_home.html

Institute for the Emotionally Intelligent: www.teacheq.com/

International Society for Humor Studies: www.hnu.edu/ishs/

Jest for the Health of It: www.jesthealth.com/frame-articles.html

Jollytologist Allen Klein: www.allenklein.com/recommend.htm

Lab for Effective Neuroscience: psyphz.psych.wisc.edu/web/index.html
Laugh Doctor: www.natural-humor-medicine.com/the-laugh-doctor.html
Layered Curriculum, by Kathie Nunley: help4teachers.com
Lenny Dave: www.creativity123.com/
Lighthouse Professional Alliance, by Susan J. Jones: www.susanjjones.com
National Institutes of Health: www.nih.gov
Paper Wad Ideas, by Scott Endres: www.paperwadideas.com/
Wavelength, Communication through Comedy: www.wavelengthinc.com/
Whole Brain Atlas, anatomy of the brain, CATs, MRIs, etc.: www.med.harvard
    .edu/AANLIB/
World Laughter Tour: www.worldlaughtertour.com/index.asp

Media

Dr. Fred Goodwin, director of the Center on Neuroscience Medical Progress
    in Society, George Washington University, and host of *The Infinite Mind* on
    National Public Radio.
Schoolhouse Rock song "Three Is a Magic Number," by Bob Dorough.

ABOUT THE AUTHOR

Mary Kay Morrison keeps looking for humor! She continues to find it while conducting workshops that link laughter and learning. In addition to humor, Mary Kay has conducted sessions on brain research, leadership, ADHD, stress management, parent education, group facilitation, and mentoring. She has been a keynote speaker for numerous college and school district events and has spoken at the National Staff Development conference and the Association for Applied and Therapeutic Humor conference. She was a team member of the Illinois State Board of Education mentor training program and participated in planning the Illinois "train the trainer" project for No Child Left Behind.

Mary Kay is an educator who has taught kindergarten through college level classes. She has a B.S. in education and an M.S. in adult education with Illinois State certification in education administration. For ten years she worked at the Boone/Winnebago Regional Office of Education to provide school improvement training for administrators in over two hundred schools. Her previous work included counseling at Kishwaukee College with the GED and teen parent program. Mary Kay is membership chair of the audience development committee for the International Association for Applied and Therapeutic Humor. She serves on the city of Rockford Early Learning Council.

Mary Kay is currently director of Humor Quest, with the goal of providing workshops on the links between humor and positive emotionality. The focus of her work for the past decade has been exploring the relationship between cognitive research, humor, and learning.

She is consistently sustained and encouraged by her husband, Don, children, their spouses, and nine grandchildren. She enjoys gardening, yoga, and biking.